T0289466

Compensating Wounded Warriors

An Analysis of Injury, Labor Market Earnings, and Disability Compensation Among Veterans of the Iraq and Afghanistan Wars

Paul Heaton, David S. Loughran, Amalia R. Miller

Prepared for the Office of the Secretary of Defense
Approved for public release; distribution unlimited

NATIONAL DEFENSE RESEARCH INSTITUTE

The research described in this report was prepared for the Office of the Secretary of Defense (OSD). The research was conducted within the RAND National Defense Research Institute, a federally funded research and development center sponsored by OSD, the Joint Staff, the Unified Combatant Commands, the Navy, the Marine Corps, the defense agencies, and the defense Intelligence Community under Contract W74V8H-06-C-0002.

Library of Congress Cataloging-in-Publication Data

Heaton, Paul, 1978-
  Compensating wounded warriors : an analysis of injury, labor market earnings, and disability compensation among veterans of the Iraq and Afghanistan wars / Paul Heaton, David S. Loughran, Amalia R. Miller.
      p. cm.
  Includes bibliographical references.
  ISBN 978-0-8330-5931-4 (pbk. : alk. paper)
  1. Disabled veterans—Employment—United States—Evaluation. 2. Disabled veterans—Services for—United States—Evaluation. 3. Afghan War, 2001---Veterans—Services for—United States. 4. Iraq War, 2003-2011—Veterans—Services for—United States. I. Loughran, David S., 1969- II. Miller, Amalia R. III. Title. IV. Title: Analysis of injury, labor market earnings, and disability compensation among veterans of the Iraq and Afghanistan wars.

UB357.H43 2012
331.2'97308697—dc23
                                                                    2012026087

Published 2012 by the RAND Corporation
1776 Main Street, P.O. Box 2138, Santa Monica, CA 90407-2138
1200 South Hayes Street, Arlington, VA 22202-5050
4570 Fifth Avenue, Suite 600, Pittsburgh, PA 15213-2665
RAND URL: http://www.rand.org/
To order RAND documents or to obtain additional information, contact
Distribution Services: Telephone: (310) 451-7002;
Fax: (310) 451-6915; Email: order@rand.org

Preface

Federal law mandates that every four years the President complete a review of the compensation system for uniformed service members. In December 2009, the President directed the Secretary of Defense to focus that review, the 11th Quadrennial Review of Military Compensation (QRMC), on four areas: (1) combat compensation; (2) Reserve Component (RC) compensation; (3) compensation for wounded warriors; and (4) pay incentives for critical career fields. The research reported here addresses compensation for wounded warriors.

Since September 11, 2001, the United States has deployed more than 1.7 million service members to support military operations in Iraq and Afghanistan. A substantial number of them have been injured while deployed in direct combat operations or as a result of other deployment-related activities. This study examines the effects of injuries sustained during Operation Enduring Freedom and Operation Iraqi Freedom (OEF/OIF) on the subsequent labor market earnings of service members and their spouses and the extent to which retirement and disability payments made by the Department of Defense (DoD), the Department of Veterans Affairs (VA), and the Social Security Administration (SSA) have compensated for lost earnings. This monograph should be of interest to policymakers, manpower analysts, and health professionals concerned about the effects of injuries sustained while deployed on the lives of veterans and their families.

This research was sponsored by the Office of the Secretary of Defense and conducted within the Forces and Resources Policy Center of the RAND National Defense Research Institute, a federally funded research and development center sponsored by the Office of the Secretary of Defense, the Joint Staff, the Unified Combatant Commands, the Navy, the Marine Corps, the defense agencies, and the defense Intelligence Community.

Comments regarding this monograph are welcome and may be addressed to David Loughran by email at david_loughran@rand.org. For information on the RAND Forces and Resources Policy Center, see http://www.rand.org/nsrd/ndri/centers/frp.html or contact the director (contact information is provided on the web page).

Contents

Figures

Tables

Summary

Nearly a decade of operational combat in Iraq and Afghanistan has focused attention on meeting the needs of military service members, especially those injured in combat, following deployment. Two recent commissions—the President's Commission on Care for America's Returning Wounded Warriors (2007) and the Veterans' Disability Benefits Commission (2007)—have recommended fundamental changes in how DoD and the VA evaluate, treat, compensate, and otherwise support injured service members and their families. To address this continuing issue, the President directed the Secretary of Defense to examine compensation benefits available to wounded warriors, caregivers, and survivors of those fallen service members as part of the 11th QRMC. In response to a request from the 11th QRMC, RAND performed the first comprehensive, quantitative assessment of how injury sustained while deployed in support of OEF/OIF affects subsequent labor market outcomes and the extent to which retirement and disability payments received from DoD, the VA, and SSA compensate for earnings losses attributable to injury. The findings of that assessment are presented in this monograph.

Study Design

The study employs data on injury, labor market earnings, and disability compensation for a large sample of Active Component (AC) and RC members deployed to Iraq and Afghanistan between September 11, 2001, and December 2006. These longitudinal, largely administrative data were obtained from DoD, the VA, and SSA and were linked by Social Security numbers. The resulting database tracks labor market earnings and disability compensation, reported in 2010 dollars, between 1998 and 2010 for nearly 700,000 service members and their spouses.

Each service member in the sample is categorized according to available self-reported and administrative data on the incidence and severity of injury sustained while deployed, as follows:

- Uninjured.
- Health worsened: The service member reported on the Post-Deployment Health Assessment (PDHA) that his or her health worsened during deployment, but the member was not referred for follow-up care.
- Referred: The service member reported on the PDHA that his or her health worsened during deployment, and the PDHA indicates that the member was referred for follow-up care.
- Non-serious casualty: The service member sustained a non–life-altering combat injury, according to official casualty data.
- Serious casualty: The service member sustained a life-altering combat injury, according to official casualty data.
- Very serious casualty: The service member sustained a life-threatening combat injury, according to official casualty data.

Approximately 18 percent of the service members in the sample reported that their health worsened during deployment; 2.7 percent sustained a non-serious combat injury; 0.2 percent sustained a serious combat injury; and 0.1 percent sustained a very serious combat injury.

We compared the labor market earnings of injured service members and their spouses in the years following deployment with the labor market earnings of uninjured service members and their spouses. Since the incidence of injury is likely to be correlated with characteristics of service members that could themselves be correlated with labor market outcomes (e.g., pay grade, military occupation, risk-taking behavior), we controlled for a rich array of individual-level characteristics, including labor market outcomes prior to deployment (i.e., we estimated such correlations in first differences). This approach eliminated the potentially confounding influence of fixed unobservable characteristics of individuals correlated with the incidence of injury and labor market outcomes, increasing the likelihood that our results can be interpreted as the causal effect of injury on earnings. However, these controls are imperfect, and the estimated correlation between injury and post-deployment labor market outcomes reported here could reflect, in part, time-varying unobserved characteristics of service members, which would undermine such a causal interpretation.

Labor Market Earnings Effects

Figure S.1 shows the estimated effect of injury on service member labor market earnings by year since the end of deployment and component. The figure demonstrates that (1) the estimated effect of less-serious injury (health worsened, referred, non-serious combat injury) on service member earnings is small, ranging from –$2,079 to –$6,080 four years following deployment (representing from 3 to 10 percent of service member earnings), whereas the estimated effect of serious and very serious combat

Figure S.1
Estimated Effect of Injury on Service Member Labor Market Earnings, by Injury Type, Years Since Deployment, and Component

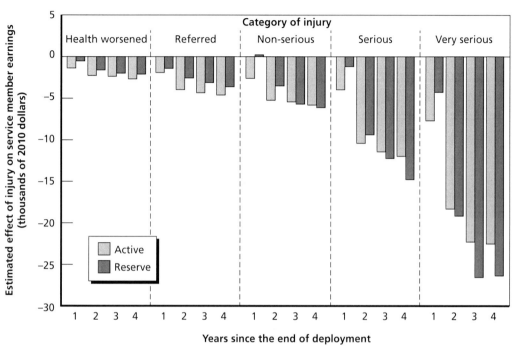

RAND *MG1166-S.1*

injury on service member earnings is quite large, ranging from –$11,943 to –$26,261 four years following deployment (between 19 and 41 percent of service member earnings); (2) the estimated negative effect of injury on earnings increases markedly over the first four years following injury; and (3) patterns of estimated earnings loss of AC and RC members are broadly similar. We can observe earnings effects as many as seven years following deployment for a part of our sample, and estimates including those service members suggest that earnings losses do not change significantly between years 4 and 7.

A significant driver of loss of labor market earnings among injured service members is a decline in earnings resulting from military separation. Figure S.2 shows that injured service members in all categories are substantially more likely to separate from the military in the years following the end of deployment and that this differential grows over time. By year 4, injured service members are estimated to be from 5 to 45 percentage points more likely to have separated from the military than uninjured service members. Thus, we believe that earnings losses increase over the first four years following deployment not because the injury itself worsens over time, but because injury eventually leads to separation from the military and such separation leads to lower labor market earnings. However, our estimates imply that serious and very

Figure S.2
Estimated Effect of Injury on Military Separation, by Injury Type, Years Since Deployment, and Component

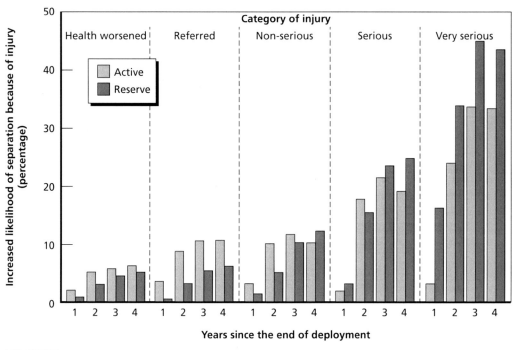

RAND *MG1166-S.2*

serious combat injury results in substantial losses in labor market earnings from civilian sources as well, especially among reservists.

The financial impact of injury may extend to the spouses of injured service members who must curtail their labor supply in order to provide care or, conversely, might increase their labor supply in an effort to offset earnings losses experienced by their injured spouses. Figure S.3 shows that serious and very serious combat injuries lower spousal labor market earnings, but the effect is quite small relative to the effect of injury on the service member's own labor market earnings (and frequently is not statistically distinguishable from zero). Very serious combat injury lowers spousal earnings by between $2,144 and $2,755 four years following deployment (from 14 to 18 percent of earnings). Point estimates imply a positive effect of less-serious injury on spousal earnings, but these estimates are small and, for the most part, statistically indistinguishable from zero.

Estimated Income Replacement Rates

Injured service members can potentially receive disability compensation from a number of sources, including DoD disability retired pay, VA disability pay, Combat-Related

Figure S.3
Estimated Effect of Injury on Spousal Labor Market Earnings, by Injury Type, Years Since Deployment, and Component

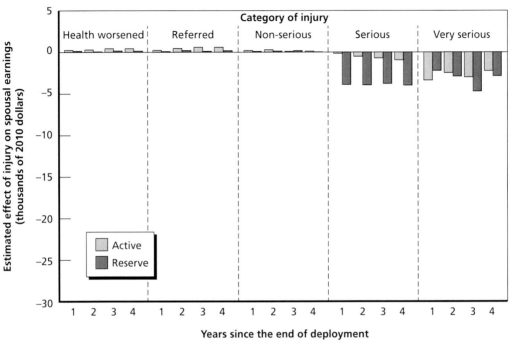

RAND MG1166-S.3

Special Compensation (CRSC), and Social Security Disability Insurance (SSDI). In addition, some injured service members are eligible to receive one-time payments from the Traumatic Servicemembers Group Life Insurance (TSGLI) program. Many of these disability payments are received tax free, which we account for in our estimates. Figure S.4 shows that, on average, these sources of compensation fully, if not more than fully, offset the estimated effect of injury on labor market earnings. The estimated effect of injury on total household income—by which we mean the sum of service member and spousal labor market earnings and disability compensation—in the fourth year following deployment is always positive among RC members (ranging from $167 to $27,780) and is positive for all but the less seriously injured AC members (from –$1,354 to $19,976). The decline in the positive effect of injury on household income between years 1 and 2 reflects the fact that one-time TSGLI payments, which range from $25,000 to $100,000, are typically made in the first year following deployment.

Table S.1 shows actual household earnings including disability payments as a percentage of expected household earnings (the replacement rate), by component, injury type, and years since deployment. Estimated replacement rates in the fourth year following deployment range from 98 to 154 percent among injured AC members and from 107 to 183 percent among injured RC members. The higher replacement rates

Figure S.4
Estimated Effect of Injury on Household Income Including Disability Compensation, by Injury Type, Years Since Deployment, and Component

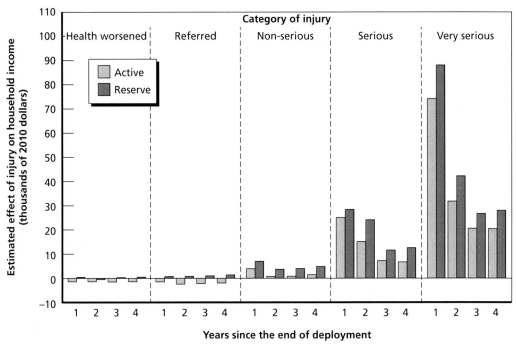

RAND *MG1166-S.4*

among injured reservists reflect their somewhat higher propensity to receive VA disability compensation and SSDI. Replacement rates are generally higher in years 1 and 2, reflecting the influence of lump-sum TSGLI payments made in those years.

Discussion

Among the many hardships of military deployment is the possibility of injury; 18 percent of deployed service members in our sample returned home feeling that their health worsened over the course of deployment, and another 3 percent were wounded in combat. This study found that combat injuries, about half of which, in our sample, resulted in a VA disability rating, decrease household labor market earnings by an average of 11 percent four years following deployment. Although estimated earnings losses are considerably lower among the less seriously injured (health worsened/referred), about 5 percent, the large numbers of service members with such injuries add significantly to the social cost of conducting the wars in Iraq and Afghanistan. Service members in our sample deployed to Iraq and Afghanistan between 2001 and 2006 and returning home with these less-serious injuries experienced aggregate labor market

Table S.1
Estimated Replacement Rates, by Injury Type, Type of Disability Compensation, and Component

Item	Injury Type				
	Health Worsened	Referred	Non-Serious Casualty	Serious Casualty	Very Serious Casualty
AC					
Household earnings loss in year 4 (2010 dollars)	2,693	4,651	5,787	11,943	22,555
Percentage of of average earnings	4	7	9	19	36
Replacement rate (percentage)					
Year 1	101	100	114	165	280
Year 2	100	97	105	146	181
Year 3	99	98	105	124	159
Year 4	99	98	105	122	154
RC					
Household earnings loss in year 4 (2010 dollars)	2,079	3,614	6,080	14,755	26,261
Percentage of of average earnings	3	4	10	22	41
Replacement rate (percentage)					
Year 1	101	110	128	186	442
Year 2	97	108	115	188	213
Year 3	107	109	113	142	182
Year 4	107	109	114	143	183

earnings losses of $1.6 billion through 2010. Official casualties, by comparison, experienced $556 million in aggregate earnings losses, according to our estimates.[1] Disability compensation paid to injured service members (over and above that paid to uninjured service members) in our sample over this same period totaled $2.3 billion—107 percent of estimated lost household earnings.

We have not attempted to answer the difficult normative question of whether the replacement rates reported here, which are well above 100 percent for those with serious combat injuries, are appropriate. Disability compensation can be viewed as a form of insurance against the possibility of injury, and elementary economic models suggest

---

[1] We compute aggregate household earnings loss by multiplying model parameter estimates by number of observations in the corresponding injury, post-deployment year, and component cell and summing over components and post-deployment years. It is important to recognize that estimated aggregate earnings losses are almost certainly a lower limit on the actual aggregate earnings losses. Although our sample is large and comprehensive, it probably omits some fraction of the individuals who were injured while deployed to Iraq and Afghanistan; thus our aggregate analysis will omit their income losses from the totals.

that risk-averse individuals demand full insurance for potential losses, which would argue for a 100-percent replacement rate. But injured service members potentially lose more than just capacity in the labor market; they may incur considerable out-of-pocket costs in adapting to their injuries, and nonpecuniary losses such as pain and suffering or loss of consortium can be significant. Economic theory also suggests that replacement rates above 100 percent can be justified for occupations in which calculated risk-taking is desirable (e.g., policing, firefighting, military service). In addition, individuals typically enjoy real wage growth, particularly early in their careers, while disability payments are indexed for inflation but typically do not otherwise increase over time. Taking a life-cycle perspective, it may be logical to provide benefits above full replacement initially to account for the fact that those with permanent disability will not enjoy the earnings growth their uninjured peers can expect.

Acknowledgments

This research would not have been possible without the assistance of dedicated staff within the Office of the Secretary of Defense, SSA, and the VA. We are especially thankful to Tom Bush, Director of the 11th QRMC; LTC Ronald Hunter, Deputy Director of the 11th QRMC; and Barbara Bicksler, Strategic Analysis, Inc., for their guidance and support throughout the project. We are indebted to Darlena Ridler and Gail Budda of the Defense Manpower Data Center; Michael Risha, Stuart Friedrich, Jim Fahlfeder, Marc Sinofsky, and Scott Muller of SSA; and Eric Robinson, Chief Inter-agency Data Sharing, and Stephen Wurtz, Deputy Director for Insurance Services, of the VA, for assisting in obtaining and interpreting the data employed in this research. We thank Jim Hosek, Beth Asch, John Winkler, Richard Buddin, and Paco Martorell, our colleagues in the RAND Forces and Resources Policy Center, for reviewing earlier presentations of this work and providing insightful comments and suggestions for this monograph. Finally, we thank Craig Martin for providing outstanding programming support.

Abbreviations

AC	Active Component
AFQT	Armed Forces Qualification Test
BAH	Basic Allowance for Housing
BAS	Basic Allowance for Subsistence
CPI-U	Consumer Price Index for All Urban Consumers
CRDP	Concurrent Retirement and Disability Pay
CRSC	Combat-Related Special Compensation
DEERS	Defense Eligibility Enrollment Reporting System
DMDC	Defense Manpower Data Center
DoD	Department of Defense
FICA	Federal Insurance Contributions Act
FSA	Family Separation Allowance
IDES	Integrated Disability Evaluation System
MBP	monthly benefit paid
MBR	SSA Master Beneficiary Record
MEB	Medical Evaluation Board
MEF	SSA Master Earnings File
OEF/OIF	Operation Enduring Freedom and Operation Iraqi Freedom
PDHA	Post-Deployment Health Assessment
PEB	Physical Evaluation Board

PTSD	post-traumatic stress disorder
QRMC	Quadrennial Review of Military Compensation
RC	Reserve Component
SGA	substantial gainful activity
SGLI	Servicemembers' Group Life Insurance
SMC	special monthly compensation
SSA	Social Security Administration
SSDI	Social Security Disability Insurance
SSN	Social Security Number
TDRL	Temporary Disability Retirement List
TSGLI	Traumatic Servicemembers' Group Life Insurance
VA	Department of Veterans Affairs
VASRD	Veterans Affairs Schedule of Rated Disabilities
WEX	DMDC Work Experience File

CHAPTER ONE

Introduction

Nearly a decade of operational combat in Iraq and Afghanistan has focused attention on meeting the needs of military service members, especially those injured in combat, following deployment. Two recent commissions—the President's Commission on Care for America's Returning Wounded Warriors (2007) and the Veterans' Disability Benefits Commission (2007)—have recommended fundamental changes in the way the Department of Defense (DoD) and the Department of Veterans Affairs (VA) evaluate, treat, compensate, and otherwise support injured service members and their families. To address this continuing issue, the President directed the Secretary of Defense to examine compensation benefits available to wounded warriors, caregivers, and survivors of those fallen service members as part of the 11th Quadrennial Review of Military Compensation (QRMC). In response to a request from the 11th QRMC, RAND performed the first comprehensive, quantitative assessment of how injury sustained while deployed in support of Operation Enduring Freedom and Operation Iraqi Freedom (OEF/OIF) affects subsequent labor market outcomes and the extent to which retirement and disability payments received from DoD, the VA, and the Social Security Administration (SSA) compensate for earnings losses attributable to injury.

According to official casualty statistics, some 43,100 U.S. military service members had been non-fatally wounded during OEF/OIF as of April 2011.[1] Many more deployed service members have incurred mental and physical injuries that are not recorded in casualty statistics but nonetheless have the potential to profoundly impact future health and well-being. Tanielian and Jaycox (2008), for example, estimate that as many as 30 percent of service members deployed in support of OEF/OIF return home suffering from post-traumatic stress disorder (PTSD), depression, and/or traumatic brain injury. Heaton and Loughran (2011) find that 8 percent of reservists deployed in support of OEF/OIF reported being hospitalized during their deployment, more than one-third complained of back pain, and nearly one-quarter reported that their health had worsened during deployment.

---

[1] Defense Manpower Data Center, undated.

While recent data-collection efforts have greatly improved our understanding of the types and frequencies of injuries service members have sustained while deployed in support of OEF/OIF,[2] we know relatively little about how these injuries impact subsequent well-being. This is especially true with respect to labor market outcomes, such as employment and earnings, which anecdotal evidence, but not necessarily rigorous research, suggests are likely to be negatively impacted by injuries sustained during deployment. Loughran and Klerman (2011) find that deployment reduces the civilian labor market earnings of military reservists by about 2 percent, on average, in the year following deployment, but this negative effect turns positive in subsequent years. Heaton and Loughran (2011) show that military reservists symptomatic of PTSD at the end of deployment experience an additional 6-percent decline in labor market earnings four years following deployment and that much of this decline is attributable to higher rates of military separation among those symptomatic of PTSD.[3]

Other recent research—for example, Buddin and Kapur (2005), Christensen et al. (2007), EconSys (2008), and Buddin and Han (2011)—shows that while the labor market earnings of veterans are negatively correlated with disability ratings assigned by DoD and the VA, disability compensation, on average, fully (if not more than fully) compensates for earnings losses attributable to disability. However, all of the prior studies note that some groups of disabled veterans appear to be less than fully compensated for lost earnings. For example, EconSys (2008) and Christensen et al. (2007) find that veterans with a disability rating of 100 percent have total earnings below those of otherwise similar veterans with no service-connected disability.

The present study, which encompasses Active Component (AC) and Reserve Component (RC) members whose deployments ended between 2003 and 2006 and follows their and their spouses' subsequent labor market and disability compensation experiences through 2010, differs from past research on injury and disability compensation in a number of significant ways.[4] First, it focuses on injury sustained during deployment rather than on having a service-connected disability. A service-connected disability could be attributable to virtually any incident while serving on active duty, requires a DoD or VA determination of disability, and results in separation from the military. By focusing on injury rather than service-connected disability, this study does

---

[2]   For information on the prevalence of mental health problems among OEF/OIF veterans, see, for example, Hoge et al., 2004; Milliken, Auchterlonie, and Hoge, 2007; and Tanielian and Jaycox, 2008.

[3]   A number of recent studies examine the effect of deployment on other outcomes such as child test scores and family stress (Lyle, 2006; Chandra et al., 2010; Werber et al., 2008), marriage and divorce (Negrusa, Negrusa, and Hosek, undated; Karney and Crown, 2007), and military reenlistment (Hosek and Martorell, 2009). See also Hosek, Kavanagh, and Miller, 2006; Tanielian and Jaycox, 2008; and Hosek, 2011, for summaries of previous studies on the effect of deployment on service member well-being.

[4]   We focus only on deployed individuals, since the purpose of this study is to estimate the effect of injury on earnings net of any other deployment-related effects; the disability compensation system compensates individuals for injury and not other hardships associated with deployment.

not condition on military separation, which by itself can independently affect earnings (Angrist, 1998; Loughran et al., 2011), or on the DoD and VA disability rating determination processes. Second, it focuses on service members injured during OEF/OIF and follows their earnings through 2010. The study population in past research on this topic is dominated by individuals separating from military service prior to OEF/OIF and whose injuries were not attributable to deployment. Third, it accounts for recent policy changes allowing for concurrent receipt of DoD and VA retirement and disability payments, the receipt of lump-sum payments for specific traumatic injuries, and Social Security Disability Insurance (SSDI) payments. Fourth, it employs longitudinal earnings data to show how the effect of injury on labor market earnings and disability compensation changes in the years following injury and to control more completely for the potentially confounding effect of differences in the characteristics of service members who do and do not incur injury. Finally, it shows how the effect of injury differs across AC and RC members and how injury affects not only their own earnings but the earnings of their spouses as well. The spouses of service members could experience declines in labor market earnings if they curtail labor supply in an effort to care for their injured husbands or wives, yet the effect of service members' injuries on the earnings of their spouses is virtually unstudied.[5]

The remainder of this monograph has the following structure. Chapter Two describes the data we employ to define our sample and measure key outcomes such as injury, labor market earnings, and disability compensation. Chapter Three presents descriptive statistics related to these outcomes. Chapter Four describes our empirical approach. Chapters Five and Six report the estimated effect of injury on labor market earnings and total household income including disability compensation, respectively. Chapter Seven discusses the aggregate labor market cost of deployment-related injury and the fraction of that cost "replaced" by existing disability-compensation mechanisms.

---

[5] Christensen et al. (2009) report an estimate of the earnings losses of the caregivers (spouses, parents, and others) for seriously wounded service members by imputing their earnings and assuming these caregivers must stop work altogether. Angrist and Johnson (2000) and Savych (2008) find deployment and other work-related absences have a small negative impact on the earnings of military spouses while the service member is away from home.

CHAPTER TWO

Data

This study draws on administrative data on injury, labor market earnings, and disability compensation obtained from DoD, the VA, and SSA. This chapter explains how we used those data to construct our analysis sample and key measures of injury and earnings.

The Sample

The initial sample for this study consists of 717,225 AC and RC members deployed to Afghanistan and Iraq who completed the Post-Deployment Health Assessment (PDHA-DD Form 2796) or who appear in the Defense Manpower Data Center's (DMDC's) Casualty File between June 1, 2003, and December 31, 2006.[1] All service members deployed outside the continental United States to a land-based location with no fixed U.S. medical treatment facility for 30 or more continuous days must complete the PDHA within five days of the end of deployment. As stated on DD Form 2796, the principal purpose of the PDHA is "to assess your state of health after deployment outside the United States in support of military operations and to assist military healthcare providers in identifying and providing present and future medical care to you." To this end, the PDHA records self-reported information about current physical and mental health and documents concerns regarding exposure to environmental toxins, viruses, and the like. The PDHA process includes a face-to-face interview with a healthcare professional, and the results of that interview are also recorded on the PDHA form, along with any referrals for follow-up medical care. While the PDHA process has existed since 1998, it was not fully implemented until 2003.[2]

To the PDHA sample we added service members who appear in the Casualty File but not in the PDHA data between June 1, 2003, and December 31, 2006. The

---

[1] The sample includes service members reporting a deployment location of Kuwait or Qatar, under the assumption that they were in fact in Iraq and/or Afghanistan during at least part of their deployment. Most deployments to these areas in our data occur in 2003 and probably reflect the pre–Iraq-invasion buildup of military forces.

[2] See Joint Chiefs of Staff, 2002.

Casualty File is the source of official statistics on U.S. casualties sustained in support of OEF/OIF. Any service member whose regular duty assignment is disrupted as a result of an injury sustained during hostile action is recorded in the Casualty File, along with information about the nature of the injury and the date it was sustained. Many of these individuals do not complete a PDHA because the seriousness of their injuries obviates the need for conducting such an assessment.[3]

For each service member in our sample, we selected the deployment with the most recent end date. In the specifications presented in the appendix, we also omitted a small number of service members (less than 0.5 percent of our sample) who appear in the Casualty File after 2006. As explained in Chapter Four, we did this so that service members in our control group, who were not injured while deployed (hereafter referred to as uninjured service members), remain uninjured (to the best of our knowledge) in the years following their last deployment between 2003 and 2006.[4]

Demographic Covariates and Spouses

Data on age, gender, component, race/ethnicity, pay grade, education, score on the Armed Forces Qualification Test (AFQT), military occupational specialty, and state of residence were obtained from DMDC's Work Experience File (WEX) and the Defense Eligibility Enrollment Reporting System (DEERS). We also employed DEERS to identify which service members were married in the year prior to deployment and the Social Security Numbers (SSNs) of their spouses. We identified 242,463 spouses of AC members and 132,820 spouses of RC members in our sample.

Beginning and end dates of deployment were obtained from self-reports in the PDHA or, for service members who appear in the Casualty File but not in the PDHA, from DMDC's Global War on Terror Contingency File.[5] Dates of separation from military service were obtained from the WEX.

Injury Categories

We employed the PDHA and Casualty File to measure injuries in our sample. Medical professionals at a field hospital or other medical treatment facility categorize service

---

[3] It is likely that some deployed service members fail to complete the PDHA for reasons other than serious injury. We have no reason to believe, however, that this incomplete coverage biases the results reported here.

[4] Of course, this selection rule might introduce other bias, since individuals who were injured after 2006 are more likely, all else equal, to have remained in the military and could possess other characteristics correlated with subsequent injury that are also correlated with labor market outcomes.

[5] The Global War on Terror Contingency File uses data provided by the services and military pay data to determine dates of deployment. We could have used this source to define our sample, but we chose to use the PDHA instead because of our desire to employ the health data recorded on it.

members who appear in the Casualty File as having non-serious (non–life-altering), serious (life-altering), or very serious (life-threatening) combat injuries, or they are counted as fatalities. For individuals who do not appear in the Casualty File, we use data on injuries referred for follow-up care and the individuals' own assessments of whether their health changed for the worse while deployed, categorizing them as

- No injury: The service member was not referred for follow-up care and did not state that his or her health worsened during deployment.
- Health worsened: The service member stated that his or her health worsened during deployment but he or she was not referred for follow-up care.[6]
- Referred: The service member stated that his or her health worsened during deployment and the injury was referred for follow-up care.

We categorized a service member as having a referred injury if the PDHA recorded a referral indicated for one or more of the following conditions: cardiac; combat/operational stress reaction; dermatological; ear, nose, and throat; eye; family problems; fatigue, malaise, multisystem complaint; audiology; gastrointestinal; genitourinary; gynecological; mental health; neurological; orthopedic; pulmonary; or other condition.

We included individuals who do not appear in the Casualty File to capture those who may have been injured while deployed but not in a manner that would lead to their inclusion in official casualty statistics. We could have categorized deployment-related injury in the PDHA in a variety of ways, but we decided that using the service member's own subjective assessment of his or her change in health in combination with indications of physician referrals was an efficient way to group such injuries. Self-reported health assessments of this sort are commonly used in studies of health and well-being and have been shown to be highly correlated with actual diagnoses, activities of daily living, and mortality in a variety of contexts (see, for example, Bound, 1991). In the PDHA, self-reported health change is correlated with other self-reported health conditions, physician referrals, and DoD disability ratings.

Our resulting injury classification is mutually exclusive, with injuries recorded in the Casualty File taking precedence over those recorded in the PDHA. We emphasize, however, that this ordering is imperfect in the sense that we cannot be certain that all injuries recorded in the Casualty File are necessarily more serious than those recorded in the PDHA. In some instances, for example, an individual might have sustained a serious injury as a result of combat actions, but circumstances did not dictate that the injury be recorded in the Casualty File. This individual would then likely be categorized as "health worsened" or "referred." As another example, psychological injuries sustained while deployed could result in a claim that health worsened or a referral but

---

[6] The specific question on the PDHA is "Did your health change during this deployment?" Respondents can choose "Health stayed about the same or got better" or "Health got worse."

could have an effect on long-term well-being as serious as or more serious than injuries recorded in the Casualty File. In theory, injuries recorded in the PDHA that lead to chronic conditions or permanent disability could have a greater effect on long-term well-being than life-threatening physical injuries from which a service member fully recovers. Despite these caveats, we refer in this monograph to serious and very serious casualties as *more severely/seriously injured* and the health worsened, referred, and non-serious casualties groups as *less severely/seriously injured*.

We use these injury categories rather than disability ratings as our primary measure of injury, because disability ratings—which reflect both the underlying injury and the outcome of the ratings process—are arguably less clearly exogenous (or unrelated to individual agency) than injuries. Individuals may differ in the way they approach the ratings process, and if those differences are related to differences in earnings potential, the estimated correlation between disability ratings and earnings will confound the effect of injury with the effect of other, non-injury factors.

To permit comparisons with prior work for some supplementary analyses, we divide service members listed in the Casualty File according to their DoD disability rating (explained below) rather than the qualitative indicator of severity found in the Casualty File. The disability rating categories used in those analyses are 0 percent, 10 to 40 percent, 50 to 70 percent, and 80 to 100 percent.

Labor Market Earnings

Our measure of labor market earnings includes cash compensation received from DoD and civilian employers. Earnings data were obtained from SSA and DMDC. SSA records in its Master Earnings File (MEF) earnings from all sources subject to Medicare taxes, including household employers and self-employment.[7] These data are considered to be of very high quality and have been used in many empirical studies, including several related to the labor market outcomes of veterans (e.g., Angrist, 1990, 1998; Christensen 2007; Loughran, Klerman, and Martin, 2006; EconSys, 2008; Loughran et al., 2011).

Not included in SSA earnings records are military allowances—e.g., Basic Allowance for Subsistence (BAS), Basic Allowance for Housing (BAH), Family Separation Allowance (FSA)—and bonuses, which are not subject to Medicare taxes. To account for these significant sources of military earnings, we add these quantities to SSA earnings, using individual-level pay records contained in DMDC's Active and Reserve Duty Pay Files. We obtained annual earnings data between 1995 and 2010 for 97 per-

---

[7] See Social Security Online, undated, for a list of employment categories that are exempt from Medicare taxes. Unlike Social Security earnings, Medicare earnings are not capped at the Social Security taxable limit.

cent of our sample, leaving 456,218 AC and 236,580 RC members in our analysis file.[8] Our file also contains spousal earnings records over the same period for 224,977 AC and 122,101 RC members. All earnings figures are deflated to 2010 dollars, using the Consumer Price Index for All Urban Consumers (CPI-U).

Disability Compensation

Injured service members are potentially eligible to receive disability compensation from DoD, the VA, and SSA. These disability benefits and the data we use to capture them are described below.

DoD Disability Retired Pay

The military services have the authority to separate service members whose injuries prevent them from performing duties consistent with their office, rank, grade, or rating. Once a service member's condition has stabilized, a Medical Evaluation Board (MEB) at a medical treatment facility makes an initial assessment of whether he or she has a medical condition that is incompatible with continued military service. MEBs then forward such cases to a Physical Evaluation Board (PEB), which makes a formal determination of fitness for duty and rates the service member's disability according to the Veterans Affairs Schedule of Rated Disabilities (VASRD). On the VASRD, disabilities are rated on a 100-point scale in 10-percentage-point increments. Unlike the VA, PEBs evaluate only conditions that compromise ability to serve in the military. Service members receive full military pay during this review process, which can take a year or more to complete, especially for injuries that do not stabilize quickly.

Service members who receive a disability rating of 30 percent or more and are deemed unfit for service are eligible to receive DoD disability retired pay, which is a function of the member's retired pay base, which is itself a function of past military earnings and either the individual's disability rating or years of service, whichever yields the highest benefit.[9] Service members who receive a disability rating of 10 or 20 percent and are not retirement-eligible are eligible to receive a disability severance payment. The value of that payment depends on pay grade, years of service, date of discharge, and whether the disability is combat-related.[10] Service members whose dis-

---

[8]   Virtually all service members should appear in the SSA data, since basic pay is subject to Medicare tax. Match rates below 100 percent, therefore, are probably due to discrepancies in the names, SSNs, and dates of birth used to match service members to SSA records.

[9]   The formula for DoD disability retired pay is retired pay base x adjustment factor, where adjustment factor is the maximum of the service member's disability rating or (years of service x 2.5)/100.

[10]   According to the Uniformed Services Almanac: "For disability separations occurring prior to January 28, 2008, the disability severance pay is computed by multiplying the monthly basic pay or the member's grade at the time of discharge or the monthly basic pay of any higher grade in which he or she served satisfactorily by twice

abilities are not considered stable are placed on the Temporary Disability Retirement List (TDRL) and are eligible to receive disability retired pay even if their disability is rated less than 30 percent. Individuals on the TDRL are reexamined periodically until their condition is deemed stable.

We obtained data on DoD retired pay (disability and non-disability) from DMDC's Retired Pay File, which records monthly retired pay for any individual receiving such pay. Disability severance data were not available for the RC, so we did not include them on our analyses in order to maintain comparability across the AC and RC. Only a small percentage of those in our sample are potentially eligible for disability severance, and the average amount for those who receive it is quite small and paid in a lump sum.

VA Disability Benefits

Service members can and frequently do obtain a separate disability rating from the VA, regardless of whether DoD considers them to be unfit for service. The VA employs the same VASRD scale to rate disabilities but considers the total effect of all service-connected disabilities that limit civilian labor market potential. These service-connected disabilities could be attributable to any aspect of active-duty service and might not be manifest until after the individual separates from the military. Thus, it is not uncommon for service members to receive different disability ratings from DoD and the VA. It also is not uncommon for an individual with identical DoD and VA disability ratings to receive different amounts of DoD disability retired pay and VA disability benefits, since VA disability benefits are not a function of the DoD retired pay structure but rather are based on a schedule intended to reflect lost civilian earnings potential.[11] VA disability benefits also vary with number of dependents, and veterans with specific types of injuries, such as loss of a hand or foot, are entitled to receive additional spe-

---

the number of years of active service. The maximum payment is two years [of] basic pay. Effective for disability separations occurring on or after January 28, 2008, the minimum years of active service for computing disability pay is six in the case of a combat-related disability and three in the case of any other disability for which this pay is being paid. The maximum payment is three yeas, two months [of] basic pay." Service members who receive disability severance must pay this amount back to DoD if they subsequently receive monthly disability benefits from the VA unless their injury was incurred in the line of duty in a combat zone or as a result of performing duty during combat-related operations.

[11] In an effort to simplify the disability rating process, DoD and the VA developed the Integrated Disability Evaluation System (IDES), first piloted in fall 2007 and now in place worldwide. DoD uses IDES to decide if injured service members are still able to serve. If they are not, IDES gives them a VA disability rating before they leave the service. IDES also helps service members file a VA benefit claim before they separate from the military and allows for informal review boards and more chances to revisit decisions during the rating process. DoD PEB liaison officers and military service coordinators from the VA guide service members through IDES. Legal counsel is also available at no cost to the service member.

cial monthly compensation (SMC) that varies with the injury and the need for specific types of medical care.[12]

For this study, we obtained from the VA a special extract of VA disability benefits (including SMC and other miscellaneous cash payments) paid to each service member in our sample between 2004 and 2010. These data include VA payments to individuals who did not receive a disability rating from DoD and so would not necessarily be recorded in DMDC's Retired Pay File.

Concurrent Retirement and Disability Pay and Combat-Related Special Compensation

Prior to OEF/OIF, DoD disability retired pay was, with few exceptions, fully offset by VA disability benefits, meaning that service members received the maximum of the two amounts. In 2004 and 2008, however, Congress enacted laws allowing for two new payments, called Concurrent Retirement and Disability Pay (CRDP) and Combat-Related Special Compensation (CRSC), which reduce the extent to which VA disability benefits offset DoD disability retired pay. CRDP, which is being phased in through 2014, is paid to service members who retire with 20 or more years of service and have a VA rated disability of at least 50 percent. CRSC, which is not subject to federal income taxes, is paid to service members who are eligible to receive DoD disability retired pay, have a VA disability rating of 10 percent or more, and can demonstrate that their VA disability rating is attributable at least in part to a combat-related injury. Service members must apply to receive CRSC, whereas DoD automatically pays CRDP to eligible individuals. Both CRDP and CRSC were included in the extract of the Retired Pay File provided to us by DMDC.

Traumatic Injury Protection Under Service Members' Group Life Insurance

Both AC and RC members are eligible to purchase life insurance through the Servicemembers' Group Life Insurance (SGLI) program administered by the VA. Service members who do not want SGLI must opt out, so the vast majority participate in the program. All of those enrolled in SGLI are automatically enrolled in the Traumatic Servicemembers' Group Life Insurance (TSGLI) program, which insures service members against the occurrence of specific traumatic injuries, including amputation, paralysis, burns, sight injury, hearing injury, facial reconstruction, coma, and traumatic brain injury.[13] TSGLI payments range from $25,000 to $100,000 depending on the injury or combination of injuries incurred. All service members participating in SGLI were made eligible for TSGLI beginning in December 2005, and at that time, coverage was made retroactive to cover injuries incurred in OEF/OIF between October 7, 2001,

---

[12] See Military.com, undated, for a complete list of conditions that qualify for SMC.

[13] See "TSGLI Schedule of Losses," undated, for a complete list of qualifying injuries and conditions.

and November 30, 2005.[14] The VA provided us with a list of all service members who had received TSGLI through May 2011, along with the dates and amounts received.

Social Security Disability Insurance

Injured service members may also be eligible to receive SSDI benefits. To obtain SSDI benefits, an individual must demonstrate that he or she has a physical or mental condition that prevents him or her from engaging in any substantial gainful activity (SGA) and that is expected to last at least 12 months or result in death. SSA defines *substantial gainful activity* as activity that results in the receipt of pay or profit of more than an established threshold (currently $1,000/month). Thus, unlike DoD and VA benefits, SSDI benefits are conditional on labor market activity. The potential loss of SSDI benefits can create a financial disincentive against (increased) labor market activity for injured service members who have work opportunities. This could lead to lower observed wage earnings associated with injury (this possibility is discussed further in Chapter Four).

SSDI beneficiaries must also be under the age of 65 and have sufficient work history, which depends on their age. Individuals who were disabled before the age of 22 and do not have sufficient work history can potentially claim SSDI benefits based on their parents' work experience.

Initial SSDI eligibility determinations require about four months to complete, on average (Office of Inspector General, 2008).[15] Individuals who are denied benefits in this initial phase can make up to four appeals; nationwide, approximately two-thirds of SSDI applicants are ultimately awarded benefits (Maestas et al., 2011). Applicants must reduce work below the SGA threshold for five months before they can receive SSDI benefits. After receiving benefits, individuals can engage in SGA above the established threshold for the first year or so; after that, benefits are suspended in months in which SGA exceeds the earnings threshold. SSDI benefits are converted to Social Security retirement benefits when the beneficiary reaches the full retirement age.

Our data on SSDI benefits come from SSA's Master Beneficiary Record (MBR) file, which records payments from all Social Security trust fund accounts to all beneficiaries. We constructed a measure of annual SSDI benefits paid to each of the service-member households in our sample by summing two sets of payments. First, we add up all payments made to any beneficiary on the service member's or spouse's account. These payments will capture SSDI benefits paid to the injured service member as well as any supplemental payments made to a spouse or children on the account. Second, to capture disability payments made to service members who became disabled during or

---

[14] Beginning in October 2011, the Veterans' Benefits Act of 2010 (PL 111-275) extends these retroactive benefits to qualifying losses incurred during this period regardless of service-member location or prior SGLI enrollment status.

[15] SSA now expedites SSDI claims made by service members injured in combat (GAO, 2009).

after their deployment but before accumulating sufficient work experience to qualify for benefits, we sum all payments made to the service member (or his or her spouse) as a beneficiary on some other person's account. In particular, an individual with a disability that started before age 22 can become entitled to SSDI "child" benefits on his or her parent's account if one of the parents is either receiving Social Security retirement or disability payments or died after having worked long enough to qualify for Social Security benefits. We do not include payments made to other beneficiaries of service members who collect benefits on another's account, such as retired parents.

Although we refer to this measure as "SSDI benefits," it actually includes any payment made from a Social Security trust fund, including the retirement trust fund. In our sample, however, a very high fraction of this total benefit amount is accounted for by SSDI benefits, since very few deployed service members are near retirement age.

We use the monthly benefit paid (MBP) amount on the MBR to compute annual SSDI benefits. MBP records show the payment amount for which the service member was eligible in a given month (we exclude monthly benefits for which the beneficiary is listed as ineligible). MBP does not necessarily reflect the actual amount paid in that month retroactively updated to reflect the correct payment eligibility after changes in status. For example, if a service member was initially denied SSDI benefits but then appealed and qualified after some delay, his or her first payment could occur several months after the initial eligibility date. Although actual payments are increased in later months to compensate for this delay, our data record payments made in each month of active eligibility. Since our data are current as of June 2011, which is more than five years after the deployment dates in our sample, and since veteran disability cases now receive priority processing at SSA, we expect the payments to be correct for most of our sample.

Tax Advantage

Military allowances, certain military pays (e.g., those received while serving in an officially designated combat zone), VA disability benefits, CRSC, TSGLI, and a portion of DoD disability retired pay and SSDI benefits are not subject to federal income, payroll, and Social Security—i.e., Federal Insurance Contributions Act (FICA)—taxes.[16] We computed the value of this federal tax advantage, assuming that service members have no interest or dividend income or capital gains, that those who are unmarried in

---

[16] DoD disability retired pay that is not offset by VA benefits is not subject to federal income taxes if the injury that resulted in retirement is combat-related. We employed an indicator variable on DMDC's Retired Pay File to determine whether the service member's disability retired pay was attributable to a combat-related injury. The taxation of SSDI benefits depends on household income; because we were unable to fully account for these tax rules, we assume that all SSDI benefits are untaxed. This is a reasonable assumption for the vast majority of injured service members in our sample, who most likely have limited financial assets.

the year prior to deployment file as single with no dependents, and that those married in the year prior to deployment file as married with one dependent child.[17] We apportioned the total value of the tax advantage to each tax-advantaged earnings/disability compensation category according to the category's proportion of total earnings and compensation.

Summary

Our final analysis sample consisted of 456,218 AC and 236,580 RC members. In the models described in Chapters Five and Six, we employed data on annual earnings and disability compensation (including an estimate of the tax advantage) for each individual in the full calendar year prior to deployment and each full calendar year following deployment through 2010. Separations from military service were measured in each calendar year following deployment. All covariates other than injury, deployment location, and military occupational specialty while deployed were measured in the year prior to deployment.

Table 2.1 presents the mean and standard deviation of the key variables in the models described in Chapters Five and Six, by component at the end of deployment. Dependent variables (outcomes) modeled include the service member's total, civilian, and military labor market earnings; whether he or she has positive labor market earnings; his or her spouse's labor market earnings; whether the spouse has positive labor market earnings; household earnings (service member plus spousal labor market earnings); and, finally, labor market earnings plus disability payments. These descriptive statistics are discussed further in Chapter Three.

---

[17] The tax imputations do not account for state taxes or state or federal earned income tax credits.

Table 2.1
Descriptive Statistics, by Component

Variable	AC	RC
Outcomes		
Annual post-deployment earnings[a]		
Own civilian earnings	10,545	29,618
Own military earnings	43,090	21,576
Own total earnings	53,636	51,194
Own total earnings > 0	0.929	0.948
Spousal earnings[b]	14,439	21,874
Spousal earnings>0[b]	0.589	0.677
Household earnings	60,742	62,466
Annual Disability Benefits[a]		
DoD retirement pay	1,132	374
DoD disability pay	50	56
VA disability benefits	1,738	1,766
CRSC	16	12
SSDI	325	675
TSGLI	131	73
Cumulative separation rate	0.297	0.270
Covariates		
Injury		
No injury	0.822	0.736
Health worsened	0.071	0.092
Referred	0.070	0.148
Non-serious casualty	0.028	0.019
Serious casualty	0.003	0.002
Very serious casualty	0.001	0.001
Death	0.005	0.003
Demographics		
Age	26.844	31.766
Female	0.106	0.108
Male	0.894	0.892
White	0.708	0.703
Black	0.186	0.148
Hispanic	0.093	0.083
Other race	0.001	0.063
Married in year prior to deployment	0.493	0.516

Table 2.1—Continued

Variable	AC	RC
No high school diploma	0.076	0.136
High school diploma	0.701	0.502
Some college	0.079	0.180
Bachelor's degree	0.105	0.124
Graduate degre	0.036	0.053
AFQT	58.401	59.020
Military service		
Army	0.629	0.812
Air Force	0.192	0.103
Navy	0.033	0.035
Marine Corps	0.146	0.050
Pay grade: junior enlsited (E-1–E-4)	0.531	0.435
Pay grade: senior enlisted (E-5+)	0.337	0.435
Pay grade: warrant Officer	0.016	0.013
Pay grade: junior Officer (O-1–O-3)	0.091	0.078
Pay grade: senior Officer (O-4+)	0.013	0.022
Pre-deployment health		
Sought mental health counseling	0.032	0.018
Have a medical problem	0.096	0.117
Currently on light duty	0.074	0.057
Self-reported health: Excellent	0.244	0.247
Self-reported health: Very good	0.291	0.335
Self-reported health: Good	0.161	0.183
Self-reported health: Fair	0.014	0.012
Self-reported health: Poor	0.001	0.001
Number of Observations		
Service members	456,218	236,580
Spouses	242,463	132,820

NOTES: Other model covariates include dummies for year deployment begins, month and year deployment ends, dummies for state of residence, dummies for miiitary occupation specialty in both the year prior to deployment and while deployed, AFQT squared, and dummies for missing education, AFQT, pay grade, and pre-deployment health variables.

[a] All earnings and benefits are reported in 2010 dollars and include an estimate of the value of the federal tax advantage.

[b] Spousal earnings are conditional on being married in the year prior to deployment.

CHAPTER THREE

Descriptive Statistics on Injury, Earnings, and Disability Compensation

The descriptive statistics on injury, labor market earnings, and disability compensation presented in this chapter help put the results reported in Chapters Five and Six in context.

Injury

Tables 3.1 and 3.2 show that about 82 percent of AC members and 74 percent of RC members in our sample returned home from deployment without injury (i.e., did not appear in the Casualty File during their deployment and did not report that their health worsened over the course of their deployment). AC members were somewhat more likely than RC members to report that their health worsened during deployment (14 versus 24 percent). Of those reporting that their health worsened, reservists were considerably more likely than AC members to be referred for follow-up medical care (15 versus 7 percent). Tables 3.1 and 3.2 also indicate that AC members are more likely to appear in the Casualty File than reservists (3.2 versus 2.1 percent). A host of factors could be responsible for the observed difference in the incidence of injury across components. Possibilities include differences in military occupation and specific deployment location that drive the risk of injury.

There appears to be a strong correlation between the qualitative assessment of injuries recorded in the Casualty File and the more formal assessment made in the DoD disability rating processes (Table 3.3). About 11 percent of those with non-serious injuries receive a DoD disability rating within four years following deployment; about 10 percent of them are medically retired within that time period, in contrast to about 35 percent and 65 percent of serious and very serious casualties. Only 2 percent of members with non–Casualty File injuries receive a DoD disability rating within four years of deployment. The percentage increases with the severity of injury, averaging 47, 52, 57, and 74 percent for non–Casualty File, non-serious, serious, and very serious casualties, respectively. However, a high percentage of uninjured (16 percent) and non–Casualty File (33 percent) individuals receive a disability rating from the VA within

Table 3.1
AC Members Injured, by Injury Categorization

Injury Category	Number	Percentage
Injury categorization 1		
No injury	375,070	82.21
Health worsened	32,189	7.06
Referred	32,079	7.03
Non-serious casualty	12,991	2.85
Serious casualty	1,287	0.28
Very serious casualty	501	0.11
Death	2,101	0.46
Injury categorization 2		
No injury	375,070	82.21
Health worsened	32,189	7.06
Referred	32,079	7.03
Casualty File: 0% disability[a]	12,499	2.74
Casualty File: 1–40% disability	879	0.19
Casualty File: 50–70% disability	856	0.19
Casualty File: 80–100% disability	545	0.12
Death	2,101	0.46

[a] Casualty File groups categorize service members who appear in the Casualty File according to their DoD disability rating.

four years of deployment. The apparent disconnect between DoD and VA disability ratings could be attributable to any number of factors, including the likelihood that some injuries sustained while deployed do not manifest debilitating symptoms until after the service member has separated from the military.

Pre-Deployment Labor Market Earnings

Table 3.4 highlights a number of interesting patterns with respect to labor market earnings prior to deployment and, hence, prior to injury. First, the pre-deployment labor market earnings of service members who subsequently appear in the Casualty File are considerably lower than those of the uninjured and non-casualties ($35,445 versus $42,114, on average). Second, individuals who receive a referral for subsequent

Table 3.2
RC Members Injured, by Injury Categorization

Injury Category	Number	Percentage
Injury categorization 1		
No injury	174,159	73.62
Health worsened	21,716	9.18
Referred	35,041	14.81
Non-serious casualty	4,562	1.93
Serious casualty	356	0.15
Very serious casualty	131	0.06
Death	615	0.26
Injury categorization 2		
No injury	174,159	73.62
Health worsened	21,716	9.18
Referred	35,041	14.81
Casualty File: 0% disability[a]	4,308	1.82
Casualty File: 1–40% disability	255	0.11
Casualty File: 50–70% disability	304	0.13
Casualty File: 80–100% disability	182	0.08
Death	615	0.26

[a] Casualty File groups categorize service members who appear in the Casualty File according to their DoD disability rating.

medical care have the highest average earnings in our sample. These two facts suggest considerable heterogeneity in the pre-deployment characteristics of injured service members that is likely to be correlated with future labor market outcomes. Although these differences in pre-deployment earnings are probably accounted for in part by differences in pay grade (which we control for in our models) and years of service, controlling for pre-deployment earnings, which we do implicitly via first-differencing, provides a more complete control for the potentially confounding effect of fixed unobserved heterogeneity. This aspect of our empirical model is explained more thoroughly in Chapter Four.

Third, as expected, civilian labor market earnings contribute little to the earnings of AC members. Reservists, on the other hand, receive about 59 percent of their total labor market earnings from civilian sources in the year prior to deployment. Fourth, although total service member labor market earnings are similar across AC and RC members, RC spouses appear to earn substantially more than AC spouses ($20,460

Table 3.3
Percentage with DoD and VA Disability Ratings Four Years Following Deployment, by Injury Type and Component

Injury Category	AC			RC		
	DoD	Mean DoD	VA	DoD	Mean DoD	VA
No injury	1	48	17	0	50	14
Health worsened	2	47	27	1	47	27
Referred	3	45	36	3	49	39
Non-serious casualty	11	52	44	10	54	55
Serious casualty	34	57	62	39	57	76
Very serious casualty	64	74	76	71	75	85

NOTES: Disability ratings and payments observed four years following deployment. DoD columns show percentage with a positive DoD disability rating. Mean DoD columns show mean DoD disability rating, conditional on having a positive disability rating. VA columns show percentage receiving a VA disability payment.

Table 3.4
Pre-Deployment Labor Market Earnings, by Injury Type and Component

Injury Category	Own Earnings			Spousal Earnings	Household Earnings
	Civilian	Military	Total		
AC					
No injury	681	41,715	42,396	11,029	47,808
Health worsened	662	41,410	42,072	11,169	47,571
Referred	701	43,312	44,013	11,003	50,057
Non-serious casualty	760	34,681	35,440	9,309	39,631
Serious casualty	714	34,811	35,526	10,329	39,491
Very serious casualty	781	34,539	35,320	9,987	39,626
RC					
No injury	24,030	17,280	41,310	20,490	51,681
Health worsened	24,340	16,692	41,032	20,660	51,725
Referred	25,960	16,106	42,066	20,469	53,730
Non-serious casualty	19,969	15,308	35,277	18,427	44,188
Serious casualty	23,607	14,275	37,882	18,567	47,583
Very serious casualty	19,404	15,354	34,758	19,876	43,710

NOTES: Earnings (in 2010 dollars) measured in the year prior to deployment. Spousal earnings are conditional on being married in the year prior to deployment.

versus $10,985, on average). This difference could be attributable to the fact that RC spouses are less likely to have moved recently due to a permanent change in station. The prospect of such moves can undermine a spouse's attachment to the labor force.

Disability Compensation

Tables 3.5 and 3.6 show the percentages of service members in our sample receiving various types of disability compensation, and Tables 3.7 and 3.8 show mean unconditional disability compensation by years since deployment and component. The tables highlight several important features of disability compensation. First, disability compensation increases markedly with years since deployment, which is unsurprising given that injuries must stabilize before they can be evaluated and the disability determination process takes time to complete. Second, disability compensation of all types increases with the severity of injury. Third, a fairly high percentage of uninjured service members are receiving DoD retirement (5 percent, on average) and VA disability (16 percent, on average) four years following deployment, and about 2 percent are receiving SSDI. Our estimates of the earnings loss replaced by disability compensation explicitly account for the fact that some uninjured also receive disability compensation. Fourth, a high percentage of serious and very serious casualties (24 percent and 53 percent, respectively) receive TSGLI payments in the first year following deployment. As shown in Tables 3.7 and 3.8, these one-time payments can be quite large. Finally, by the fourth year following deployment, injured RC members in our sample were somewhat more likely to receive VA disability compensation and SSDI than were injured AC members. As will be shown in Chapter Six, this difference in disability compensation across components, which we cannot explain with our data, drives considerable differences in estimated replacement rates.

Table 3.5
Percentage of AC Members Receiving Disability Compensation, by Injury Type and Years Since Deployment

Injury Category	Disability Compensation Type					
	DoD Retirement	DoD Disability	VA Disability	CRSC	SSDI	TSGLI
No injury						
Year 1	2.1	0.1	4.0	0.0	0.5	0.0
Year 2	3.4	0.3	8.3	0.0	0.8	0.1
Year 3	4.9	0.5	13.3	0.1	1.2	0.1
Year 4	6.3	0.7	17.2	0.2	1.6	0.1
Health worsened						
Year 1	3.4	0.3	8.2	0.0	0.7	0.0
Year 2	5.0	0.6	15.1	0.1	1.2	0.1
Year 3	6.7	0.9	21.8	0.2	1.8	0.1
Year 4	8.2	1.1	27.0	0.3	2.4	0.1
Referred						
Year 1	4.9	0.7	12.7	0.0	1.1	0.0
Year 2	6.8	1.2	22.5	0.2	2.0	0.1
Year 3	8.9	1.5	30.0	0.4	3.0	0.1
Year 4	10.7	1.6	35.6	0.7	4.0	0.1
Non-serious casualty						
Year 1	0.7	2.7	15.3	0.1	3.5	5.3
Year 2	1.1	3.6	29.0	0.6	5.2	2.5
Year 3	1.7	3.3	38.4	2.1	6.7	1.2
Year 4	2.2	3.1	43.9	3.5	7.8	0.6
Serious casualty						
Year 1	0.8	10.3	23.9	0.1	11.1	24.7
Year 2	1.3	10.2	45.7	1.5	13.2	14.0
Year 3	1.9	7.6	57.8	4.7	14.5	3.7
Year 4	2.4	5.8	62.2	8.7	15.9	1.6
Very serious casualty						
Year 1	0.6	12.2	33.7	0.0	39	53.3
Year 2	0.6	14.0	59.5	4.2	41.1	17.4
Year 3	1.2	8.4	72.1	14.6	43.5	4.2
Year 4	1.2	6.2	75.8	25.1	42.7	1.4

Table 3.6
Percentage of RC Members Receiving Disability Compensation, by Injury Type and Years Since Deployment

Injury Category	Disability Compensation Type					
	DoD Retirement	DoD Disability	VA Disability	CRSC	SSDI	TSGLI
No injury						
Year 1	0.6	0.0	6.1	0.0	1.2	0.0
Year 2	1.1	0.1	9.2	0.0	1.6	0.0
Year 3	1.7	0.2	11.6	0.1	2.2	0.0
Year 4	2.3	0.3	14.0	0.1	2.9	0.0
Health worsened						
Year 1	0.8	0.4	13.6	0.0	2.0	0.1
Year 2	1.4	0.6	20.3	0.1	2.9	0.0
Year 3	2.0	0.7	24.5	0.2	4.0	0.0
Year 4	2.6	0.9	27.4	0.3	5.1	0.0
Referred						
Year 1	0.9	0.5	20.1	0.0	3.0	0.1
Year 2	1.6	1.1	30.5	0.1	4.5	0.1
Year 3	2.2	1.3	35.8	0.2	6.2	0.1
Year 4	3.0	1.5	39.3	0.5	7.8	0.0
Non-serious casualty						
Year 1	0.4	2.6	27.7	0.0	5.7	4.5
Year 2	0.6	3.7	44.0	0.3	8.1	1.5
Year 3	0.7	3.6	51.5	1.6	10.4	1.1
Year 4	0.9	3.4	55.4	3.3	11.4	0.9
Serious casualty						
Year 1	0.3	10.4	38.5	0.0	18.3	20.2
Year 2	0.0	12.6	63.5	0.6	22.5	14.6
Year 3	1.1	11.0	71.6	5.3	23.6	2.2
Year 4	1.1	9.6	75.6	13.2	25.0	3.4
Very serious casualty						
Year 1	0.0	17.6	49.6	0.0	41.2	52.7
Year 2	0.0	14.5	77.1	3.1	47.3	16.0
Year 3	0.0	8.4	86.3	18.3	46.6	3.1
Year 4	0.0	8.4	84.7	29.8	44.3	4.6

Table 3.7
Mean Disability Compensation for AC Members, by Injury Type and Years Since Deployment (in 2010 dollars)

Injury Category	Disability Compensation Type					
	DoD Retirement	DoD Disability	VA Disability	CRSC	SSDI	TSGLI
No injury						
Year 1	343	5	170	0	62	25
Year 2	707	19	577	2	111	49
Year 3	1,027	36	1,124	5	187	43
Year 4	1,356	51	1,782	11	275	50
Health worsened						
Year 1	552	20	398	1	88	50
Year 2	963	43	1,242	5	170	56
Year 3	1,283	68	2,177	10	301	81
Year 4	1,595	91	3,221	19	442	49
Referred						
Year 1	726	41	670	2	149	42
Year 2	1,256	88	2,121	12	301	65
Year 3	1,601	119	3,493	36	519	61
Year 4	1,956	138	4,870	59	757	45
Non-serious casualty						
Year 1	117	131	1,126	2	546	4,808
Year 2	199	226	3,597	27	892	2,179
Year 3	277	248	5,864	103	1,237	752
Year 4	370	234	7,646	197	1,507	317
Serious casualty						
Year 1	114	559	3,375	6	1,824	23,338
Year 2	201	726	9,507	33	2,431	13,705
Year 3	304	635	13,740	190	2,788	2,941
Year 4	362	463	16,506	389	3,070	839
Very serious casualty						
Year 1	110	684	9,393	0	6,809	65,282
Year 2	86	1,149	22,103	238	8,091	19,647
Year 3	101	1,042	30,193	840	8,444	4,114
Year 4	158	837	33,673	1,419	8,621	995

Table 3.8
Mean Disability Compensation for RC Members, by Injury Type and Years Since Deployment (in 2010 dollars)

Injury Category	DoD Retirement	DoD Disability	VA Disability	CRSC	SSDI	TSGLI
No injury						
Year 1	96	4	258	0	170	7
Year 2	211	11	578	1	253	22
Year 3	335	19	938	3	381	28
Year 4	464	34	1,332	8	542	21
Health worsened						
Year 1	132	25	703	1	309	38
Year 2	257	65	1,664	3	488	31
Year 3	385	73	2,569	10	739	35
Year 4	480	93	3,356	20	1,015	37
Referred						
Year 1	124	39	1,103	1	457	34
Year 2	267	104	2,610	3	800	57
Year 3	385	153	4,021	12	1,197	52
Year 4	498	190	5,226	33	1,618	37
Non-serious casualty						
Year 1	80	177	2,019	0	1,078	4,209
Year 2	120	335	5,242	12	1,709	1,328
Year 3	130	414	8,351	57	2,249	692
Year 4	163	421	10,266	166	2,627	381
Serious casualty						
Year 1	6	627	5,769	0	3,928	19,841
Year 2	0	1,227	13,307	2	4,764	15,718
Year 3	19	970	18,102	151	5,257	1,414
Year 4	76	850	20,925	523	5,729	2,215
Very serious casualty						
Year 1	0	1,283	16,849	0	8,595	66,838
Year 2	0	1,595	29,755	18	10,302	21,296
Year 3	0	1,086	38,831	699	10,381	4,582
Year 4	0	1,037	41,379	1,618	10,064	3,169

CHAPTER FOUR

Empirical Model

To estimate the causal effect of deployment-related injury on earnings and other labor market outcomes, we must first estimate the labor market outcomes that injured service members would have had if they had never been injured. To do this, we use the outcomes of similarly situated service members who were also deployed but who were not injured (i.e., the control group). The causal effect of injury is the difference between the observed labor market outcomes of injured service members and these estimated counterfactual outcomes.

To interpret this difference as the effect of injury on labor market outcomes, we must assume that such differences cannot be explained by other factors that are correlated with labor market outcomes. In general, this assumption is likely to fail. The incidence of injury is likely to be correlated with a wide range of characteristics of service members that determine their exposure to the likelihood of injury or their propensity to report that their health worsened during deployment, such as military occupation and attitudes toward risk, which also independently affect success in the labor market. The principal empirical challenge, therefore, is to control for such characteristics so that the resulting conditional correlation of injury and labor market outcomes is uninfluenced by them (in the language of econometrics, we need to solve the problem of omitted-variables bias).

We employ an empirical model that controls for fixed characteristics of service members potentially correlated with injury and earnings and allows for the possibility that differences in earnings growth over time may be a function of observable differences in these characteristics:

$$\Delta y_{it} = \beta Injury_i + \gamma X_i + \varepsilon_i \tag{1}$$

where Δy_{it} is the change in earnings experienced by individual i between the year immediately prior to deployment and the year following deployment t,[1] $Injury_i$ indicates a

---

[1]   Because our earnings data are based on a calendar year but deployments typically begin or end midyear, we use the first complete calendar year immediately prior to the start of deployment and the calendar year prior to the end date of deployment for the purpose of earnings measurement. We include fixed effects for end month of

vector of indicator variables capturing the nature of individual i's deployment-related injuries (using the injury categories described previously), X_i is a set of covariates, ε_i is an idiosyncratic error term, and $\hat{\beta}$ measures the estimated effect of injury on earnings.

A key feature of Equation 1 is the use of earnings changes rather than earnings levels as the outcome of interest. By subtracting out earnings in the pre-deployment year, we account for preexisting differences in earnings between those who ultimately sustain an injury and those who do not. One potential concern with estimating such equations is the possibility that earnings are correlated with unobserved individual characteristics—for example, risk-taking attitudes—that are also correlated with injury. This unobserved heterogeneity in earnings potential could lead to biased estimates of the impact of injury on earnings. However, if the heterogeneity largely results from differences across individuals that are fixed over time, the use of a differenced earnings measure will result in unbiased estimates.

To illustrate how using a differenced earnings measure helps to resolve bias arising from individual heterogeneity, suppose there is an individual earnings component, u_i, that persists over time, so that earnings levels in year t can be expressed as

$$Y_{it} = \ddot{y}_{it} + u_i. \tag{2}$$

Regression estimates that use Y_{it} as an outcome will be subject to omitted-variables bias if they fail to account for u_i and if u_i is correlated with any other determinants of individual earnings ($\ddot{y}_{it}$). However, this problem does not arise when using differenced earnings as an outcome, because the individual earnings component is eliminated as

$$\Delta y_{it} = Y_{it} - Y_{i0} = \ddot{y}_{it} + u_i - \left(\ddot{y}_{i0} + u_i \right) = \ddot{y}_{it} - \ddot{y}_{i0}. \tag{3}$$

However, even with differenced earnings outcomes as the dependent variable, Equation 1 may yield biased estimates of the impact of injury on earnings if there are uncontrolled factors related to injury that affect individual earnings trajectories rather than just earnings levels. To examine the empirical relevance of this potential departure from our assumptions, we plot average earnings trajectories for AC and RC members in the years immediately prior to deployment, by injury status following deployment, in Figures 4.1 and 4.2, respectively. As in Table 3.4, the figures demonstrate that there are important differences in average earnings *levels* across those who ultimately sustain different types of injury; in particular, average earnings among official casualties are appreciably below those of the uninjured or those with only self-reported injuries. While it is likely that some of these differences can be explained by observable characteristics such as military rank, years of service, and occupation, observable

---

deployment and for pre- and post-deployment calendar years to account for differences across individuals in the time between redeployment and the calendar year in which earnings are measured.

Figure 4.1
Trends in AC Pre-Deployment Earnings, by Injury Type and Years Prior to Deployment

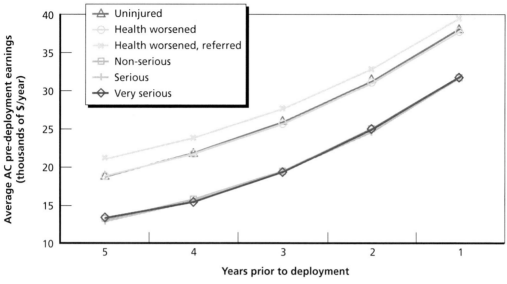

Figure 4.2
Trends in RC Pre-Deployment Earnings, by Injury Type and Years Prior to Deployment

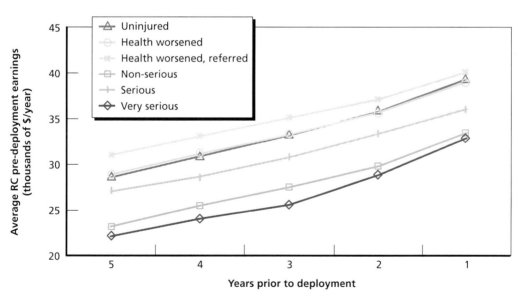

characteristics are unlikely to fully account for them, suggesting that our first-differencing approach offers a more complete solution to the problem of controlling for fixed heterogeneity than would the inclusion of demographic controls alone.

Figures 4.1 and 4.2 suggest that pre-deployment earnings trajectories are very similar across injury categories for both the AC and the RC. This suggests that pre-deployment earnings heterogeneity can largely be explained by factors that are fixed over time. We test this hypothesis formally by estimating a version of Equation 1 in which the outcome variable is the average yearly change in earnings between the fifth year prior to deployment and the year immediately preceding deployment. As can be seen in Table 4.1, most of the estimated coefficients on our injury-category dummies are not statistically different from zero despite our large sample size, and all of the estimated coefficients are small relative to earnings levels or annual earnings changes. This suggests that bias arising from the failure of the statistical assumptions underlying Equation 1 is likely to be minimal.

The potential for unobserved heterogeneity in earnings trajectories to bias estimates from Equation 1 is further mitigated by the inclusion of a wide range of controls (X_i). (See Table 2.1 for a complete list of these control variables.) A large body of research literature dating from Mincer, 1974, demonstrates a relationship between demographic characteristics—work experience and education, in particular—and earnings growth. Thus, we include in X_i a range of demographic characteristics, including age and age-squared, gender, race (white, African-American, or Hispanic), and educational attainment. Given that exposure to injury and earnings potential may differ across individuals with varying job assignments, we also control for pre-deployment rank and military occupation (36 categories). To account for potential business-cycle effects and regional economic conditions, we control for deployment end date and state of residence. Finally, we have access to data on a range of individual-level characteristics that could be correlated with earnings growth but that are typically unavailable to

Table 4.1
Estimated Effect of Injury on Pre-Deployment Annual Earnings Growth, by Injury Type and Component (in 2010 dollars)

Component	Average Uninjured	Injury Type				
		Health Worsened	Referred	Non-Serious Casualty	Serious Casualty	Very Serious Casualty
Active	4,848	83**	118**	172**	127	−11
		(17)	(18)	(26)	(85)	(125)
Reserve	2,693	−39	−97**	−22	−255	−143
		(32)	(28)	(65)	(194)	(319)

NOTES: Dependent variable is average yearly change in earnings between the fifth year prior to deployment and the year immediately preceding deployment. Model includes all covariates employed in main analyses. Heteroskedasticity-robust standard errors are in parentheses; *denotes statistical significance at the 5-percent level; ** denotes statistical significance at the 1-percent level.

researchers estimating earnings equations. These characteristics include scores on the AFQT—an achievement test designed to measure general aptitude—and several measures of pre-deployment health, including indicators for whether the service member had recently sought mental health treatment or had reported medical problems and self-rated pre-deployment health.[2] The inclusion of controls capturing pre-deployment health accounts for the possibility that some of the differences in earnings growth between the injured and uninjured could reflect health problems that existed prior to injury.

To properly measure the effects of injury on earnings, we assume that after conditioning on our control variables, idiosyncratic fluctuations in earnings, ε_i, are uncorrelated with injury status. We use differenced earnings and numerous controls to account for many possible avenues through which this assumption may fail. Nevertheless, there may be unobserved factors related to injury that also affect earnings growth, in which case our estimates might overstate or understate the true causal impact of injury on earnings.

Unlike prior studies of DoD and VA disability compensation, our control group includes the universe of service members who were deployed over our sample time frame, regardless of whether they ultimately were redeployed or remained in the military. This approach is equivalent to assuming that the future military career characteristics of the injured would have, on average, approximated those of the uninjured if no injury had occurred. Many prior studies (e.g., Greenberg and Rosenheck, 2007) compare injured veterans to uninjured veterans who are no longer in the military. One drawback of limiting such comparisons to service members who have separated from the military is that those who separate may be a nonrepresentative subset of the total force, and their earnings experience may therefore be a poor counterfactual for the earnings experience of injured service members who may or may not have separated had they not been injured.

Equation 1 incorporates both the direct effect of injury on earnings due to changes in productive capabilities and any participation effects that arise as a result of the disability compensation system. In theory, the availability of disability compensation could affect the labor market decisions of injured service members in two ways. First, the system might directly induce workers to withdraw from the labor force in order to qualify for disability payments. In our context, this possibility is relevant only for SSDI, which makes payments solely to individuals who work less than an established threshold (see Chapter Two). Second, disability compensation provides injured service members with unearned income, which, in theory, can lower labor supply irrespective of injury (more wealth induces individuals to consume more leisure and thus supply less labor). This is relevant for DoD and VA disability payments, which are largely not

---

[2]   These pre-deployment health variables were obtained from the Pre-Deployment Health Assessment (DD Form 2795) administered by DoD to approximately 74 percent of our sample.

conditional on labor market earnings.[3] Prior research suggests that the availability of disability benefits induces at least some individuals to work less than they otherwise would (e.g., Bound and Burkhauser, 1999). Our approach cannot disentangle such incentive effects from the more direct effect of injury on productive capacity. This distinction is important for understanding how readily our results might generalize to other environments with different rules governing disability payments. In particular, in environments offering disability benefits substantially above or below current levels, it is possible that we would observe patterns of earnings loss that vary from those documented here.

We conclude this section by noting several potential problems with the use of the health measures derived from the PDHA. First, we measure health at the end of deployment, but the effect of some injuries may manifest itself only at a later date, in which case our control group might include some individuals who would claim that their health worsened during deployment if they had been questioned at a later point in time. This might be particularly important for psychological injuries such as PTSD, which research has shown can develop many years after injury (McFarlane, 2000). There is little that we can do to address this possibility, since we do not have access to information about the course of injury in the post-deployment years; we therefore admit that our estimates could understate the impact of injury to the extent that such latent injuries lower earnings in the control group years after deployment has ended.

Second, some service members may be reluctant to report that their health worsened during deployment or that they were experiencing some adverse health symptom that could lead to a referral for follow-up medical care for fear that doing so would compromise their military careers. While such self-reporting bias could bias our estimates of the effect of injury, the effect the bias would have is not clear. On one hand, our control group would be contaminated with individuals who are in fact injured, which would tend to bias estimates toward zero. On the other hand, individuals who do report that their health worsened during deployment might be more seriously injured than the universe of individuals who reported that their health worsened during deployment in the absence of fear of reprisal, which would tend to bias our estimates away from zero. Thus, the net effect of self-reporting bias is not known a priori.

---

[3] Some individuals who receive a disability rating of less than 100 percent from the VA can receive benefits at the 100-percent level if they can demonstrate that they are unable to engage in "substantially gainful employment." In these cases, VA disability compensation is conditioned on labor supply in the same way that SSDI is.

CHAPTER FIVE

The Effect of Injury on Earnings and Other Labor Market Outcomes

This chapter presents the results of estimating Equation 1 (see Chapter Four) for a variety of labor market outcomes measured in the first four years following deployment for all service members in our sample. We begin by estimating the effect of injury on household (service member plus spouse) labor market earnings. We then show that effects on household earnings predominantly concern service member earnings rather spousal earnings. For AC members, the decline in earnings attributable to injury is primarily caused by a decline in military earnings, which, in turn, is due to elevated levels of military separation. Injury has substantially negative effects on both the military and civilian earnings of reservists. Finally, we show that the estimated earnings effects are partly attributable to a decline in employment (which is measured by having positive labor market earnings). The results of a variety of specification checks, including examining earnings effects through seven years following deployment and categorizing Casualty File injuries according to DoD disability ratings, are given in Appendix A.

Household Labor Market Earnings

The estimated effects of injury on various measures of individual and household (service member plus spouse) labor market earnings are reported in separate tables for each outcome and component. From the perspective of military compensation policy, these estimates are valuable because they are relatively invariant to the particular set of disability policies and programs in place at a particular moment in time.[1] They thus provide positive guidance regarding the amount of compensation needed to replace lost earnings over time among those with different levels of injury, in contrast to the normative question of how disability compensation should be structured. The estimated effect (i.e., $\hat{\beta}$ in Equation 1) is the difference in earnings growth since the year prior to deployment between injured and uninjured service members after factors related to

---

[1]   They are not completely invariant, because of the incentive effects described above.

both injury propensity and earnings growth potential are controlled for. Assuming that first-differencing and the inclusion of other controls adequately address the potential for omitted-variables bias, the estimates can be interpreted as the difference between actual earnings and the earnings that injured service members would have expected had they not been injured. Because their labor market experiences and opportunities are fundamentally different, we estimate separate models for AC and RC members.

Tables 5.1 and 5.2 show that deployment-related injury substantially lowers household earnings for both AC and RC members.[2] Since annual household earnings in the post-deployment period average around $60,000 (see Table 2.1), a $1,000 earnings loss represents roughly 1.7 percent of earnings. In these and the subsequent tables in this chapter, comparing numbers across columns shows how the effects vary with injury severity; comparing entries across rows shows how the effects evolve over time.

For both AC and RC members, the magnitude of losses increases with injury severity. For AC members, a self-reported decline in health results in an earnings loss of $1,414 in the first year. The loss is greater for the referred group ($1,993) and even greater for serious ($3,977) and very serious ($7,680) injuries. For RC members, earnings losses are smaller in the first year after deployment: A decline in self-reported health results in an earnings loss of $397, and a referral results in a loss of $386. The estimated earnings losses for less-serious casualties are not statistically significant in the first year, although the point estimate for very serious injuries is substantial (−$4,911) and statistically significant.

Table 5.1
Estimated Effect of Injury on AC Household Labor Market Earnings, by Injury Type and Years Since Deployment (in 2010 dollars)

Year After Deployment	Injury Type				
	Health Worsened	Referred	Non-Serious Casualty	Serious Casualty	Very Serious Casualty
1	−1,414** (134)	−1,993** (142)	−2,518** (202)	−3,977** (603)	−7,680** (1,032)
2	−2,229** (163)	−3,952** (173)	−5,233** (246)	−10,466** (756)	−18,328** (1,351)
3	−2,391** (175)	−4,340** (185)	−5,411** (265)	−11,447** (829)	−22,292** (1,419)
4	−2,693** (191)	−4,651** (200)	−5,787** (287)	−11,943** (893)	−22,555** (1,476)

NOTES: Heteroskedasticity-robust standard errors are in parentheses; * denotes statistical significance at the 5-percent level, ** denotes statistical significance at the 1-percent level.

---

[2] The tables in this chapter and the next present estimated coefficients for the injury variables only. Full regression results corresponding to Tables 5.1 and 5.2 are given in Tables A.1 and A.2 in the appendix.

Table 5.2
Estimated Effect of Injury on RC Household Labor Market Earnings, by Injury Type and Years Since Deployment (in 2010 dollars)

Year After Deployment	Injury Type				
	Health Worsened	Referred	Non-Serious Casualty	Serious Casualty	Very Serious Casualty
1	–397*	–386**	–126	–1,123	–4,911*
	(157)	(131)	(318)	(1,191)	(2,129)
2	–1,448**	–1,563**	–3,741**	–9,448**	–19,709**
	(183)	(153)	(372)	(1,394)	(2,377)
3	–1,770**	–2,136**	–5,937**	–12,279**	–27,138**
	(207)	(173)	(430)	(1,560)	(2,519)
4	–1,900**	–2,607**	–6,290**	–14,770**	–26,808**
	(228)	(191)	(478)	(1,707)	(2,741)

NOTES: Heteroskedasticity-robust standard errors are in parentheses; * denotes statistical significance at the 5-percent level; ** denotes statistical significance at the 1-percent level.

The estimates for different years after deployment show the time pattern of the effects of injury and distinguish short-run and longer-run impacts. Estimated earnings losses grow substantially between the first two years following the end of deployment and then grow more slowly between years 2 and 4. The sample does not change with years since deployment (i.e., it is fully balanced), so the time pattern is independent of the composition of the sample.

The growth in estimated earnings losses is more pronounced among reservists than among AC members. In the first year after deployment, the estimated effect of injury on earnings is relatively small and not always statistically insignificant. However, in year 2, the effects are negative and large across all injury categories. The estimated effects in year 1 may be smaller because of higher military compensation for injured reservists who receive medical treatment over an extended period. During that time, reservists continue to receive active-duty and combat pay, which they would no longer have received had they not been injured and ended their deployments.[3] As we will show, the growth in earnings loss between years 1 and 2 among AC members is also probably due to a decline in military earnings attributable to separation.

By year 4, the effects of injury on household earnings are comparable between the components. Those with less-severe injuries are slightly more negatively affected in the AC than in the RC, whereas the converse holds among the more severely injured.

---

[3]   There is a relative increase in the number of active-duty days in the year following deployment for reservists with referrals (61 days) and those in the Casualty File with non-serious (65 days), serious (109 days), and very serious (238 days) injuries, relative to those without reported injuries (51 days). This is particularly striking in light of the results in Table 5.12 (p. 42) that show a relative increase in separation rates for injured reservists in the first year after deployment.

Service Member and Spousal Earnings

In this study, we observed earnings effects for injured individuals and their spouses separately. While injury would be expected to have a negative impact on the injured individual's earnings, the expected impact on spousal earnings is ambiguous (e.g., Gronau, 1977). One potential response to the loss of productive capacity resulting from an injury is for spouses to increase their labor in order to maintain household earnings. This would lead to higher spousal earnings even as household earnings decline. Alternatively, spouses may withdraw from the labor force in order to care for wounded family members, compounding service-member earnings loss with decreases in spousal earnings.

We measure marital status in the year prior to deployment and do not condition our estimates on marital status following deployment, since that status could be determined in part by injury. Thus, injury could affect spousal earnings both directly through the mechanisms described above and indirectly through changes in marital status (e.g., injury may induce divorce, which often leads to higher spousal earnings). The effects on spousal earnings that we report account for both of these situations, although the relatively low incidence of divorce suggests that the dominant effect is not through changes in marital status.

Tables 5.3 through 5.6 present estimates of the effect of injury on own and spousal earnings by component. AC members experience large own-earnings losses (Table 5.3) that exhibit patterns similar to those for overall household earnings (Table 5.1). A different pattern emerges for AC spouses (Table 5.4). Spouses of service members with less-serious injury, such as self-reported adverse health changes, actually increase their earnings by a modest but statistically significant amount, and these earnings gains increase through the fourth year following deployment. For example, spouses of AC members referred for treatment earned $674 more in year 4 than did spouses of the uninjured. The reason for these earnings gains is unclear, but a variety of plausible mechanisms could explain them.[4]

For spouses of AC members with non-serious and serious injuries, the estimated effect of injury on earnings is negative but statistically insignificant. However, spouses of very seriously injured AC members experience earnings losses of several thousand dollars that begin in year 1 and remain fairly stable over time.

Tables 5.5 and 5.6 show analogous results for reservists. We do not observe strong evidence of spousal-earnings gains for any injury category, but we do observe earnings

---

[4] For example, spouses of those with minor injuries may work more to compensate for earnings losses of their spouses or to qualify for medical benefits (such as psychological counseling) provided by their own employers that may benefit their spouses. Interpersonal difficulties with a service member confronting psychological illness might induce a spouse to substitute work time for time at home. Alternatively, spouses of the uninjured may have higher fertility, leading them to substitute time at home for time at work and decreasing their relative earnings.

Table 5.3
Estimated Effect of Injury on AC Service Member Labor Market Earnings, by Injury Type and Years Since Deployment (in 2010 dollars)

Year After Deployment	Injury Type				
	Health Worsened	Referred	Non-Serious Casualty	Serious Casualty	Very Serious Casualty
1	−1,542**	−2,148**	−2,646**	−3,943**	−6,249**
	(123)	(131)	(189)	(562)	(910)
2	−2,375**	−4,257**	−5,421**	−10,304**	−17,300**
	(153)	(161)	(232)	(717)	(1250)
3	−2,616**	−4,740**	−5,518**	−11,121**	−21,033**
	(163)	(172)	(250)	(795)	(1325)
4	−2,890**	−5,085**	−5,903**	−11,515**	−21,611**
	(179)	(185)	(271)	(856)	(1,384)

NOTES: Heteroskedasticity-robust standard errors are in parentheses; * denotes statistical significance at the 5-percent level; ** denotes statistical significance at the 1-percent level.

Table 5.4
Estimated Effect of Injury on AC Spousal Labor Market Earnings, by Injury Type and Years Since Deployment (in 2010 dollars)

Year After Deployment	Injury Type				
	Health Worsened	Referred	Non-Serious Casualty	Serious Casualty	Very Serious Casualty
1	251*	236*	245	−88	−3,305**
	(107)	(103)	(162)	(600)	(830)
2	296*	472**	344	−318	−2,353**
	(121)	(118)	(186)	(677)	(881)
3	468**	626**	142	−653	−2,856**
	(134)	(130)	(201)	(719)	(955)
4	427**	674**	151	−870	−2,144*
	(144)	(139)	(222)	(736)	(1,087)

NOTES: Heteroskedasticity-robust standard errors are in parentheses; * denotes statistical significance at the 5-percent level; ** denotes statistical significance at the 1-percent level.

losses of around $4,000 per year among spouses of RC members with serious injuries. The point estimates for the spouses of the very seriously injured are large but statistically insignificant.

To summarize, we find that a very high percentage of estimated household earnings losses attributable to injury are due to declines in service member earnings. However, there is evidence of significant earnings losses among the spouses of the most seriously injured and small earnings gains among the spouses of less seriously injured AC members.

Table 5.5
Estimated Effect of Injury on RC Service Member Labor Market Earnings, by Injury Type and Years Since Deployment (in 2010 dollars)

Year After Deployment	Injury Type				
	Health Worsened	Referred	Non-Serious Casualty	Serious Casualty	Very Serious Casualty
1	−433**	−400**	−123	892	−3,974
	(141)	(116)	(288)	(1,071)	(2,045)
2	−1,442**	−1,713**	−3,816**	−7,451**	−18,465**
	(165)	(137)	(338)	(1,244)	(2,143)
3	−1,823**	−2,278**	−6,017**	−10,342**	−25,020**
	(188)	(156)	(394)	(1,379)	(2,192)
4	−1,965**	−2,762**	−6,288**	−12,808**	−25,576**
	(207)	(173)	(431)	(1,512)	(2,239)

NOTES: Heteroskedasticity-robust standard errors are in parentheses; * denotes statistical significance at the 5-percent level; ** denotes statistical significance at the 1-percent level.

Table 5.6
Estimated Effect of Injury on RC Spousal Labor Market Earnings, by Injury Type and Years Since Deployment (in 2010 dollars)

Year After Deployment	Injury Type				
	Health Worsened	Referred	Non-Serious Casualty	Serious Casualty	Very Serious Casualty
1	62	−27	−20	−3,867**	−2,103
	(134)	(106)	(283)	(997)	(2,129)
2	−18	187	150	−3,805**	−2,765
	(154)	(120)	(322)	(1,139)	(2,460)
3	95	158	160	−3,707**	−4,616
	(169)	(133)	(362)	(1,223)	(2,795)
4	119	170	−13	−3,807**	−2,755
	(185)	(143)	(401)	(1,289)	(3,619)

NOTES: Heteroskedasticity-robust standard errors are in parentheses; * denotes statistical significance at the 5-percent level; ** denotes statistical significance at the 1-percent level.

Civilian and Military Earnings

The extent to which the large own-earnings effects shown in Tables 5.3 and 5.5 attributable to declines in military as opposed to civilian earnings is important because it provides insights into the civilian labor market prospects of injured service members. Tables 5.7 and 5.8 show the estimated effect of injury on the civilian and military earnings of AC service members. Tables 5.9 and 5.10 report comparable estimates for RC members. Almost all the earnings losses of AC members, even the most seriously injured, can be explained by reductions in military earnings. The negative effect

Table 5.7
Estimated Effect of Injury on AC Member Civilian Labor Market Earnings, by Injury Type and Years Since Deployment (in 2010 dollars)

Year After Deployment	Injury Type				
	Health Worsened	Referred	Non-Serious Casualty	Serious Casualty	Very Serious Casualty
1	931**	1,338**	642**	225	−1,594**
	(75)	(80)	(98)	(264)	(310)
2	1481**	2,234**	1,252**	−83	−1,998**
	(110)	(116)	(147)	(407)	(529)
3	1644**	2,475**	1,132**	118	−2,174**
	(132)	(138)	(180)	(523)	(767)
4	1789**	2,382**	651**	−323	−2,586**
	(151)	(155)	(202)	(623)	(901)

NOTES: Heteroskedasticity-robust standard errors are in parentheses; * denotes statistical significance at the 5-percent level; ** denotes statistical significance at the 1-percent level.

Table 5.8
Estimated Effect of Injury on AC Military Earnings, by Injury Type and Years Since Deployment (in 2010 dollars)

Year After Deployment	Injury Type				
	Health Worsened	Referred	Non-Serious Casualty	Serious Casualty	Very Serious Casualty
1	−2,473**	−3,487**	−3,287**	−4,168**	−4,655**
	(149)	(157)	(223)	(622)	(970)
2	−3,856**	−6,491**	−6,673**	−10,221**	−15,301**
	(192)	(201)	(280)	(792)	(1,311)
3	−4,260**	−7,214**	−6,650**	−11,239**	−18,859**
	(203)	(211)	(294)	(884)	(1,371)
4	−4,679**	−7,467**	−6,554**	−11,192**	−19,024**
	(216)	(223)	(311)	(917)	(1,426)

NOTES: Heteroskedasticity-robust standard errors are in parentheses; * denotes statistical significance at the 5-percent level; ** denotes statistical significance at the 1-percent level.

of injury on military earnings increases markedly between years 1 and 2, especially among serious and very serious casualties. This pattern makes sense given that the military services do not evaluate whether service members can continue to serve until their injuries have stabilized, which can take some time. The estimates imply that non-serious injury actually leads to higher civilian earnings that partially offset the negative effect of such injury on military earnings. These patterns might be expected if those with less-serious injuries are more likely to separate from the military and transition into civilian employment than are the uninjured.

Table 5.9
Estimated Effect of Injury on RC Member Civilian Labor Market Earnings, by Injury Type and Years Since Deployment (in 2010 dollars)

Year After Deployment	Injury Type				
	Health Worsened	Referred	Non-Serious Casualty	Serious Casualty	Very Serious Casualty
1	−346** (134)	−1,287** (112)	−2,784** (274)	−8,106** (1,036)	−12,005** (1,547)
2	163 (157)	−394** (131)	−1,460** (318)	−6,127** (1,037)	−12,810** (1,998)
3	261 (178)	−319* (148)	−1,201** (363)	−5,293** (1,175)	−11,905** (2,109)
4	142 (196)	−347* (163)	−720 (398)	−5,296** (1,281)	−11,477** (2,174)

NOTES: Heteroskedasticity-robust standard errors are in parentheses; * denotes statistical significance at the 5-percent level; ** denotes statistical significance at the 1-percent level.

Table 5.10
Estimated Effect of Injury on RC Military Earnings, by Injury Type and Years Since Deployment (in 2010 dollars)

Year After Deployment	Injury Type				
	Health Worsened	Referred	Non-Serious Casualty	Serious Casualty	Very Serious Casualty
1	−87 (160)	887** (133)	2,661** (343)	8,998** (1,350)	8,032** (2,039)
2	−1,605** (181)	−1,319** (150)	−2,356** (360)	−1,323 (1,316)	−5,655* (2,266)
3	−2,084** (203)	−1,960** (169)	−4,816** (396)	−5,049** (1,339)	−13,115** (2,064)
4	−2,108** (220)	−2,415** (183)	−5,568** (423)	−7,512** (1,316)	−14,099** (2,000)

NOTES: Heteroskedasticity-robust standard errors are in parentheses; * denotes statistical significance at the 5-percent level; ** denotes statistical significance at the 1-percent level.

Civilian earnings losses are substantial among the more seriously injured reservists (Table 5.9), but for all but the very seriously injured, these effects decline over time (especially between years 1 and 2). For those with very serious injuries, civilian earnings losses remain fairly stable over time at around $12,000 per year.

The estimated effect of injury on the military earnings of reservists (Table 5.10) is positive in year 1 for all injury categories except reported worsening of health during deployment without referral for follow-up medical care. Military earnings effects turn negative in year 2 and become increasingly negative in subsequent years. In contrast to year 4 earnings losses of AC personnel, which are largely explained by declines in military earnings, the total earnings losses of RC members are accounted for by declines in both military and civilian earnings.

The overall pattern in Tables 5.9 and 5.10 is consistent with injured reservists remaining on active duty in the year following deployment, possibly receiving treatment for their injuries. Their civilian earnings decline, but their military earnings increase relative to those of uninjured reservists, most of whom return to work in the civilian sector. By year 2, however, the productivity impacts of their injuries begin to be manifest in both their civilian and military work.

Military Separation Rates

Our analysis thus far has revealed patterns of earnings gains and losses that might be explained in part by differential rates of military separation. In particular, earnings loss increases over time among all injury categories, which might be expected if military service in general has a positive effect on earnings (Loughran, Klerman, and Martin, 2006; Loughran et al., 2011), but separation is more likely over time among the injured. In this section, therefore, we estimate the effect of injury on cumulative separation rates in the first four years following deployment.[5]

The second column of Tables 5.11 and 5.12 shows that few uninjured service members (less than 10 percent) separate in the first year following deployment. However, cumulative separation rates for the uninjured increase substantially over the next three years. By year 4, about one-third of uninjured service members have separated.

Table 5.11
Estimated Effect of Injury on AC Members' Cumulative Military Separation Rate, by Injury Type and Years Since Deployment

| Year After Deployment | Average Uninjured | Injury Type | | | | |
		Health Worsened	Referred	Non-Serious Casualty	Serious Casualty	Very Serious Casualty
1	0.079	0.018** (0.002)	0.034** (0.002)	0.031** (0.003)	0.017* (0.008)	0.029* (0.014)
2	0.194	0.050** (0.002)	0.086** (0.003)	0.098** (0.004)	0.177** (0.013)	0.238** (0.022)
3	0.287	0.057** (0.003)	0.104** (0.003)	0.115** (0.004)	0.212** (0.013)	0.336** (0.021)
4	0.367	0.060** (0.003)	0.104** (0.003)	0.101** (0.004)	0.189** (0.013)	0.331** (0.018)

NOTES: Heteroskedasticity-robust standard errors are in parentheses; * denotes statistical significance at the 5-percent level; ** denotes statistical significance at the 1-percent level.

---

[5] Here using differenced outcomes is equivalent to examining separation rates in levels since everyone in the sample is, by definition, serving in the military prior to deployment.

Table 5.12
Estimated Effect of Injury on RC Members' Cumulative Military Separation Rate, by Injury Type and Years Since Deployment

Year After Deployment	Average Uninjured	Injury Type				
		Health Worsened	Referred	Non-Serious Casualty	Serious Casualty	Very Serious Casualty
1	0.059	0.006** (0.002)	0.004** (0.002)	0.013** (0.004)	0.029 (0.016)	0.161** (0.035)
2	0.165	0.029** (0.003)	0.030** (0.002)	0.050** (0.006)	0.153** (0.025)	0.338** (0.042)
3	0.253	0.043** (0.003)	0.052** (0.003)	0.101** (0.007)	0.234** (0.027)	0.449** (0.037)
4	0.334	0.051** (0.003)	0.061** (0.003)	0.120** (0.007)	0.247** (0.025)	0.435** (0.032)

NOTES: Heteroskedasticity-robust standard errors are in parentheses; * denotes statistical significance at the 5-percent level; ** denotes statistical significance at the 1-percent level.

Individuals with injuries are considerably more likely to separate following deployment. Their separation rates are slightly higher in the first year, and they increase substantially by year 2. The differential impact of injury on separation rates increases with injury severity; by year 4, service members with serious and very serious injuries are more than 50 percent more likely to have separated than uninjured service members. Again, the effect of less-serious injuries on separation is larger among AC members, but the effect of more-serious injury is greater among RC members.

Service Member and Spousal Labor Force Participation

In this section, we investigate whether injury affects not only earnings but also labor force participation (which we measure in our data as having positive earnings). In theory, injury could lower earnings by promoting withdrawal from the labor force or by lowering the wages of those who work, or both. Understanding the ways in which injury impacts earnings can inform disability compensation policy by, for example, providing relevant data for determining the proper mix of cash compensation and in-kind programmatic offerings such as job training.

Tables 5.13 and 5.14 present estimates of the impact of injury on labor force participation of AC members and their spouses.[6] In Table 5.13, labor force participation rates for uninjured AC members range from 99 percent in the first year following

---

[6] Since all service members are in the military prior to deployment, use of differenced labor force participation measures is equivalent to estimation in levels for the service members themselves. As with our other outcomes, we take differences between pre-deployment spousal labor force participation and post-deployment participation in order to account for any preexisting differences in propensity to work across injury categories.

Table 5.13
Estimated Effect of Injury on AC Service Member Labor Force Participation Rate, by Injury Type and Years Since Deployment

Year After Deployment	Average Uninjured	Injury Type				
		Health Worsened	Referred	Non-Serious Casualty	Serious Casualty	Very Serious Casualty
1	0.989	−0.004** (0.001)	−0.008** (0.001)	−0.008** (0.001)	−0.004 (0.004)	−0.047** (0.011)
2	0.966	−0.012** (0.001)	−0.023** (0.001)	−0.034** (0.002)	−0.088** (0.009)	−0.203** (0.019)
3	0.946	−0.019** (0.002)	−0.033** (0.002)	−0.060** (0.003)	−0.149** (0.011)	−0.332** (0.022)
4	0.920	−0.024** (0.002)	−0.041** (0.002)	−0.069** (0.003)	−0.165** (0.012)	−0.379** (0.022)

NOTES: Heteroskedasticity-robust standard errors are in parentheses; * denotes statistical significance at the 5-percent level; ** denotes statistical significance at the 1-percent level.

Table 5.14
Estimated Effect of Injury on AC Spousal Labor Force Participation Rate, by Injury Type and Years Since Deployment

Year After Deployment	Average Uninjured	Injury Type				
		Health Worsened	Referred	Non-Serious Casualty	Serious Casualty	Very Serious Casualty
1	0.598	−0.001 (0.004)	0.007 (0.004)	0.010 (0.007)	0.013 (0.022)	−0.086* (0.034)
2	0.602	0.001 (0.004)	0.013** (0.004)	0.012 (0.007)	0.044* (0.022)	−0.024 (0.034)
3	0.599	−0.001 (0.004)	0.012** (0.004)	0.005 (0.007)	0.021 (0.023)	−0.065 (0.034)
4	0.583	−0.002 (0.004)	0.011** (0.004)	0.008 (0.007)	0.001 (0.022)	−0.067 (0.037)

NOTES: Heteroskedasticity-robust standard errors are in parentheses; * denotes statistical significance at the 5-percent level; ** denotes statistical significance at the 1-percent level.

deployment to 92 percent in year 4. This is not surprising given that many of the uninjured remain in the military at least initially; as a growing fraction separate over time (Table 5.11), the labor force participation rate begins to approach that observed in the civilian labor market.

Although the uninjured experience statistically significant reductions in labor force participation that grow over time, overall participation rates remain high, and differences across injury categories are modest. A sizable fraction of those with non-serious and serious injuries remain in the labor force four years after the end of their deployment. Rates of labor force withdrawal of individuals with very serious injuries are more than twice as large as those with serious injuries. As noted previously, the extent to which these differences reflect the effects of physical impairment versus income effects arising from higher disability payments is unknown.

Roughly 60 percent of spouses of uninjured AC members participate in the labor force, a proportion that remains relatively stable following the end of deployment. In general, we observe few statistically significant differences in labor force participation among AC spouses across injury categories (Table 5.14).

Tables 5.15 and 5.16 show the effect of injury on labor force participation among RC members and their spouses. Employment patterns of RC members across injury categories are similar to those of AC members. In particular, those with less-serious injuries experience small labor force participation impacts, but those in the most severe injury category have substantial labor force participation effects.

Table 5.16 shows that spouses of reservists are slightly more likely to participate in the labor market than are spouses of AC members. Whereas we did not observe statistically significant spousal labor supply effects for even the most seriously injured AC service members, spouses of serious or very serious RC casualties reduce their labor supply substantially beginning in year 1. The estimated impacts for the very seriously injured, while only marginally statistically significant, are large, representing a roughly 15-percent reduction in labor supply.

Summary

This chapter presents an empirical model for estimating the impact of injury on labor market outcomes and reported estimates of the impacts of injury on labor market earnings, military separation rates, and labor force participation. A key advantage of

Table 5.15
Estimated Effect of Injury on RC Service Member Labor Force Participation Rate, by Injury Type and Years Since Deployment

Year After Deployment	Average Uninjured	Injury Type				
		Health Worsened	Referred	Non-Serious Casualty	Serious Casualty	Very Serious Casualty
1	0.992	−0.004** (0.001)	−0.003** (0.001)	−0.006** (0.002)	−0.017 (0.009)	−0.114** (0.030)
2	0.979	−0.012** (0.001)	−0.013** (0.001)	−0.030** (0.003)	−0.091** (0.017)	−0.251** (0.040)
3	0.967	−0.019** (0.002)	−0.026** (0.001)	−0.062** (0.004)	−0.159** (0.021)	−0.411** (0.043)
4	0.950	−0.025** (0.002)	−0.036** (0.002)	−0.084** (0.005)	−0.199** (0.023)	−0.420** (0.043)

NOTES: Heteroskedasticity-robust standard errors are in parentheses; * denotes statistical significance at the 5-percent level; ** denotes statistical significance at the 1-percent level.

Table 5.16
Estimated Effect of Injury on RC Spousal Labor Force Participation Rate, by Injury Type and Years Since Deployment

Year After Deployment	Average Uninjured	Injury Type				
		Health Worsened	Referred	Non-Serious Casualty	Serious Casualty	Very Serious Casualty
1	0.706	0.001	−0.003	−0.008	−0.101**	−0.088
		(0.004)	(0.003)	(0.009)	(0.029)	(0.054)
2	0.705	−0.004	0.000	−0.012	−0.065*	−0.104
		(0.004)	(0.003)	(0.009)	(0.033)	(0.056)
3	0.694	−0.005	−0.004	−0.003	−0.098**	−0.027
		(0.004)	(0.003)	(0.009)	(0.032)	(0.058)
4	0.670	−0.004	−0.005	−0.007	−0.090**	−0.101
		(0.004)	(0.003)	(0.010)	(0.032)	(0.072)

NOTES: Heteroskedasticity-robust standard errors are in parentheses; * denotes statistical significance at the 5-percent level; ** denotes statistical significance at the 1-percent level.

our modeling approach is the use of differenced outcome measures, which accounts for unobserved heterogeneity across individuals who ultimately suffer injury and those who do not. We further control for a wide range of demographic characteristics and present evidence based on pre-deployment earnings trends that the assumption of exogeneity of injury in this model is reasonable.

We find that household earnings losses among injured service members increase over time and with injury severity. For AC members with a referral, for example, earnings losses increase from 3 to 7 percent between years 1 and 4, compared with an increase of 13 to 36 percent among very serious casualties. Percentages of earnings losses are relatively high among less seriously injured AC members and among more seriously injured RC members.

Among both AC and RC members, household labor market earnings losses can largely be explained by declines in service member earnings, but there are statistically significant and practically important declines in the earnings of the spouses of seriously injured service members, which are partly attributable to withdrawal from the labor force.

Earnings losses of AC members can be largely explained by declines in military rather than civilian earnings, and these, in turn, can be linked to higher-than-expected separation rates from the military for the injured and general withdrawal from the labor force for the most seriously injured. For less seriously injured AC personnel, higher civilian earnings actually offset some military earnings losses.

Reservists have a more complicated story. We observe general labor force withdrawal for the most seriously injured, but injured reservists remain on active duty longer than uninjured reservists, leading to differential military and civilian earnings patterns in the first post-deployment year relative to later years. Both military and civilian earnings of injured RC members decline in later years.

CHAPTER SIX

The Effect of Injury on Household Income Including Disability Compensation

In this chapter, we estimate the extent to which retirement and disability compensation offsets the estimated household earnings losses reported in Chapter Five. We use the same empirical strategy described in Chapter Four (i.e., Equation 1), but we use changes in total household income, which we define to be the sum of household labor market earnings and retirement and disability compensation, as the dependent variable. To show the relative importance of different types of retirement and disability compensation, we sequentially add in those payments to household labor market earnings in four stages. We first add DoD and VA retirement and disability payments, then CRSC, then SSDI, and finally, TSGLI. The relevant baseline household labor market earnings losses for these comparisons are those given in Tables 5.1 and 5.2.

Effect of Injury on Household Income

We first show the estimated effect of injury on household labor market earnings, taking into account retirement and disability payments made by DoD and the VA but excluding CRSC. As can be seen in Table 6.1, these payments alone substantially offset estimated household labor market earnings losses among AC members. In many cases, the income losses are now, in fact, income gains.

The table also shows that average DoD and VA payments to injured service members increase over the four years after deployment and increase across injury categories. Service members with injuries receive, on average, between $1,216 and $31,928 of additional DoD and VA compensation in the fourth year after their deployment. These payments reduce estimated income loss in year 4 by about half for those self-reporting declines in health (55 percent for those without referrals and 48 percent for those with referrals) and fully compensate for the estimated earnings losses of non-serious casualties. DoD and VA retirement and disability payments, on average, more than fully compensate AC members with very serious injuries for estimated earnings losses. The estimates imply that those with very serious injuries receive $9,373 more in total household income in year 4 than they would have received had they not been injured.

Table 6.1
Estimated Effect of Injury on AC Household Income, Including DoD and VA Disability and Retired Pay, by Injury Type and Years Since Deployment (in 2010 dollars)

Year After Deployment	Injury Type				
	Health Worsened	Referred	Non-Serious Casualty	Serious Casualty	Very Serious Casualty
1	−1,113**	−1,456**	−1,467**	−(257)	2,239*
	(130)	(137)	(195)	(573)	(994)
2	−1,574**	−2,552**	−2,198**	−(1,068)	4,088**
	(156)	(162)	(230)	(721)	(1,292)
3	−1,436**	−2,355**	−900**	(1,300)	7,280**
	(167)	(173)	(246)	(778)	(1,377)
4	−1,477**	−2,243**	−(435)	2,456**	9,373**
	(181)	(186)	(264)	(844)	(1,438)

NOTES: Heteroskedasticity-robust standard errors are in parentheses; * denotes statistical significance at the 5-percent level; ** denotes statistical significance at the 1-percent level.

DoD and VA payments provide even greater replacement for labor market earnings for RC members, as shown in Table 6.2. These payments generally fully compensate for the estimated earnings losses, starting in the first year after deployment. RC members who report that their health worsened during deployment but are not referred for further care are the only group whose net household income declines. This decline is largest in year 2 after deployment, at $488. In other years, the decline is smaller and not statistically distinguishable from zero. For all other injury types, the receipt of DoD and VA retirement and disability payments results in net increases in total household income. These gains decline from year 1 to year 2 and then increase

Table 6.2
Estimated Effect of Injury on RC Household Income, Including DoD and VA Disability and Retired Pay, by Injury Type and Years Since Deployment (in 2010 dollars)

Year After Deployment	Injury Type				
	Health Worsened	Referred	Non-Serious Casualty	Serious Casualty	Very Serious Casualty
1	−3	281*	1,705**	4,880**	12,935**
	(155)	(130)	(311)	(1,147)	(2,387)
2	−488**	126	886*	4,040**	10,841**
	(179)	(150)	(361)	(1,401)	(2,705)
3	−350	414*	1,201**	5,113**	11,377**
	(201)	(167)	(410)	(1,541)	(2,944)
4	−202	550**	2,118**	4,673**	13,561**
	(220)	(182)	(452)	(1,692)	(3,231)

NOTES: Heteroskedasticity-robust standard errors are in parentheses; * denotes statistical significance at the 5-percent level; ** denotes statistical significance at the 1-percent level.

through year 4, at which point they range from $550 for those with referrals to $13,351 for those with very serious injuries.

The incremental effect of adding CRSC to household income is small, as shown in Tables 6.3 and 6.4. The net increase attributable to CRSC is larger in later years and for more-severe injuries, though it generally averages less than $100. For AC members with very serious injuries, CRSC adds $837 in year 3 and $1,408 in year 4 (Table 6.3). Increases in household income attributable to CRSC are similar for RC members (Table 6.4). The relatively small effect of CRSC is not surprising, since only a small percentage of injured service members in our sample receive these payments (see Tables 3.5 and 3.6).

Table 6.3
Estimated Effect of Injury on AC Household Income, Including DoD and VA Disability and Retired Pay and CRSC, by Injury Type and Years Since Deployment (in 2010 dollars)

Year After Deployment	Injury Type				
	Health Worsened	Referred	Non-Serious Casualty	Serious Casualty	Very Serious Casualty
1	−1,113**	−1,455**	−1,465**	−(251)	2,240*
	(130)	(137)	(195)	(573)	(994)
2	−1,573**	−2,545**	−2,170**	−(1,034)	4,326**
	(156)	(162)	(230)	(719)	(1,292)
3	−1,434**	−2,333**	−801**	(1,488)	8,117**
	(167)	(173)	(246)	(778)	(1,375)
4	−1,474**	−2,206**	−249	2,840**	10,781**
	(181)	(186)	(264)	(847)	(1,428)

NOTES: Heteroskedasticity-robust standard errors are in parentheses; * denotes statistical significance at the 5-percent level; ** denotes statistical significance at the 1-percent level.

Table 6.4
Estimated Effect of Injury on RC Household Income, Including DoD and VA Disability and Retired Pay and CRSC, by Injury Type and Years Since Deployment (in 2010 dollars)

Year After Deployment	Injury Type				
	Health Worsened	Referred	Non-Serious Casualty	Serious Casualty	Very Serious Casualty
1	−2	281*	1,705**	4,880**	12,935**
	(155)	(130)	(311)	(1,147)	(2,387)
2	−486**	128	896*	4,041**	10,858**
	(179)	(150)	(362)	(1,401)	(2,706)
3	−345	420*	1,252**	5,260**	12,073**
	(201)	(167)	(411)	(1,545)	(2,924)
4	−194	566**	2,272**	5,185**	15,173**
	(220)	(182)	(453)	(1,692)	(3,182)

NOTES: Heteroskedasticity-robust standard errors are in parentheses; * denotes statistical significance at the 5-percent level; ** denotes statistical significance at the 1-percent level.

Tables 6.5 and 6.6 show the effect on household income when SSDI and other SSA payments are included. For AC members, the income losses associated with injury are further reduced for those with less-severe injuries, and income gains are larger for those with more-severe injuries. The addition of SSA payments renders earnings losses for AC non-serious casualties statistically insignificant by year 3 and changes the small income loss of $249 in year 4 to a statistically significant $869 income gain. A similar pattern is evident among reservists (Table 6.6). By year 4, RC members in every injury group experience an increase in total household income relative to what they would have received in the absence of injury. Income losses persist only for reservists who

Table 6.5
Estimated Effect of Injury on AC Household Income, Including DoD and VA Disability and Retired Pay, CRSC, and SSDI, by Injury Type and Years Since Deployment (in 2010 dollars)

Year After Deployment	Injury Type				
	Health Worsened	Referred	Non-Serious Casualty	Serious Casualty	Very Serious Casualty
1	−1,096**	−1,418**	−957**	1,556**	9,032**
	(130)	(137)	(197)	(596)	(1,080)
2	−1,532**	−2,426**	−1,401**	1,317	12,323**
	(155)	(162)	(231)	(750)	(1,382)
3	−1,351**	−2,103**	181	4,093**	16,349**
	(166)	(172)	(247)	(808)	(1,459)
4	−1,353**	−1,861**	869**	5,622**	19,068**
	(180)	(185)	(265)	(870)	(1,503)

NOTES: Heteroskedasticity-robust standard errors are in parentheses; * denotes statistical significance at the 5-percent level; ** denotes statistical significance at the 1-percent level.

Table 6.6
Estimated Effect of Injury on RC Household Income, Including DoD and VA Disability and Retired Pay, CRSC, and SSDI, by Injury Type and Years Since Deployment (in 2010 dollars)

Year After Deployment	Injury Type				
	Health Worsened	Referred	Non-Serious Casualty	Serious Casualty	Very Serious Casualty
1	96	437**	2,581**	8,555**	21,348**
	(155)	(130)	(321)	(1,315)	(2,738)
2	−313	491**	2,286**	8,416**	20,875**
	(179)	(149)	(369)	(1,551)	(2,981)
3	−79	976**	3,012**	9,963**	22,040**
	(200)	(166)	(414)	(1,636)	(3,186)
4	150	1,286**	4,204**	10,149**	24,662**
	(219)	(181)	(454)	(1,753)	(3,421)

NOTES: Heteroskedasticity-robust standard errors are in parentheses; * denotes statistical significance at the 5-percent level; ** denotes statistical significance at the 1-percent level.

report a decline in health (without referral), and those losses are small and statistically insignificant, appearing only in years 2 and 3.

Finally, Tables 6.7 and 6.8 show the effect of including TSGLI payments. As might be expected, these one-time payments have a large impact on average household income losses in the year the payments are made—typically, the first year following injury. In our sample, the 2003 and 2004 deployment cohorts might have received TSGLI payments somewhat later, since they were not distributed until December 2005 (see Tables 3.5 and 3.6). For both components, these payments have a negligible effect

Table 6.7
Estimated Effect of Injury on AC Household Income, Including DoD and VA Disability and Retired Pay, CRSC, SSDI, and TSGLI, by Injury Type and Years Since Deployment (in 2010 dollars)

Year After Deployment	Injury Type				
	Health Worsened	Referred	Non-Serious Casualty	Serious Casualty	Very Serious Casualty
1	−1,067**	−1,402**	3,717**	24,824**	74,144**
	(131)	(137)	(291)	(1,482)	(3,387)
2	−1,525**	−2,397**	627*	14,746**	31,748**
	(156)	(163)	(270)	(1,356)	(2,603)
3	−1,318**	−2,086**	853**	6,972**	20,381**
	(167)	(173)	(258)	(972)	(1,794)
4	−1,354**	−1,863**	1,102**	6,381**	19,976**
	(181)	(186)	(269)	(894)	(1,540)

NOTES: Heteroskedasticity-robust standard errors are in parentheses; * denotes statistical significance at the 5-percent level; ** denotes statistical significance at the 1-percent level.

Table 6.8
Estimated Effect of Injury on RC Household Income, Including DoD and VA Disability and Retired Pay, CRSC, SSDI, and TSGLI, by Injury Type and Years Since Deployment (in 2010 dollars)

Year After Deployment	Injury Type				
	Health Worsened	Referred	Non-Serious Casualty	Serious Casualty	Very Serious Casualty
1	136	485**	6,697**	28,357**	88,049**
	(156)	(130)	(475)	(2,810)	(7,419)
2	−312	507**	3,574**	24,021**	42,089**
	(179)	(150)	(416)	(3,031)	(5,239)
3	−73	1,001**	3,662**	11,356**	26,583**
	(201)	(167)	(432)	(1,750)	(4,155)
4	167	1,301**	4,550**	12,337**	27,780**
	(220)	(182)	(461)	(1,954)	(3,734)

NOTES: Heteroskedasticity-robust standard errors are in parentheses; * denotes statistical significance at the 5-percent level; ** denotes statistical significance at the 1-percent level.

on the income of those with self-reported health changes (with or without referrals). Among serious and very serious casualties, however, the effect of TSGLI payments is very large in years 1 and 2 (the payments range from about $13,000 to $23,000 for serious casualties and $19,000 to $67,000 for very serious casualties). Even for non-serious casualties, TSLGI payments in years 1 and 2 are more than $1,000—enough to eliminate the net earnings losses of AC members. As expected, though, by years 3 and 4, most TSGLI payments have been made, so the effects of TSGLI on household income are much smaller.

Estimated Replacement Rates

The estimates in this chapter demonstrate the important role of disability compensation from both military and nonmilitary sources in supplementing the income of injured service members. One measure of the extent to which disability payments compensate for lost earnings is the so-called *replacement rate*, which we define as the ratio of actual household income including disability payments to expected household income in the absence of injury. Thus, if a service member (and spouse) had $30,000 in earned income and received $20,000 in disability payments in a given post-deployment year but would have earned $55,000 had he or she not been injured, then the estimated replacement rate for him or her would be 91 percent—i.e., ($20,000 + $30,000)/$55,000. We computed expected household income for each service member in each post-deployment year by adding the predicted increase in household income from the regression model described in Chapter Four to actual household income in the pre-deployment year, ignoring the parameter estimates for injury. Expected household income is the household income our regression model predicts a service member would have earned in a given post-deployment year had he or she not been injured. A decline in household income relative to expected household income results in a replacement rate of less than 100 percent; an increase results in a replacement rate of more than 100 percent.

Table 6.9 shows that average replacement rates are consistently near or above 100 percent and that replacement rates generally increase with the severity of injury.[1] AC members with serious and very serious injuries have replacement rates in year 4 of 122 and 154 percent, respectively. Table 6.9 also shows that average replacement rates for RC members are generally higher than those for AC members. Replacement rates in year 4 for seriously and very seriously injured RC members are 143 and 183 percent, respectively. The relatively high replacement rates among reservists are explained by relatively high average disability payments for the injured (and relatively low average

---

[1] See Appendix B for tabulations of the full distribution of replacement rates by component, injury type, and years since deployment.

Table 6.9
Estimated Replacement Rates, by Injury Type and Type of Disability Compensation

Item	Injury Type				
	Health Worsened	Referred	Non-Serious Casualty	Serious Casualty	Very Serious Casualty
AC					
Household earnings loss in year 4 (2010 dollars)	2,693	4,651	5,787	11,943	22,555
Percentage of average earnings	4	7	9	19	36
Replacement rate (percentage)					
Year 1	101	100	114	165	280
Year 2	100	97	105	146	181
Year 3	99	98	105	124	159
Year 4	99	98	105	122	154
RC					
Household earnings loss in year 4 (2010 dollars)	2,079	3,614	6,080	14,755	26,261
Percentage of average earnings	3	4	10	22	41
Replacement rate (percentage)					
Year 1	101	110	128	186	442
Year 2	97	108	115	188	213
Year 2	107	109	113	142	182
Year 4	107	109	114	143	183

disability payments for the uninjured), but why reservists receive higher disability payments on average than AC members within the same injury category in our sample is not known. Finally, the table shows that replacement rates are generally higher in years 1 and 2, reflecting the influence of lump-sum TSGLI payments made in those years.

Discussion

Among the many hardships of military deployment is the possibility of injury; 18 percent of deployed service members in our sample returned home feeling that their health worsened over the course of deployment, and another 3 percent were wounded in combat. These more-serious combat injuries, about half of which result in a VA disability rating in our sample, decrease household labor market earnings by an average of 11 percent four years following deployment. Although estimated earnings losses are considerably lower among those with a self-reported decline in health but no combat injuries, the relatively large numbers of such service members add significantly to the social cost of conducting the wars in Iraq and Afghanistan. Table 7.1 shows that service members in our sample who were deployed to Iraq and Afghanistan between 2001 and 2006 and returned home with these less-serious injuries experienced aggregate labor market earnings losses of $1.6 billion through 2010. Official casualties, by comparison, experienced aggregate earnings losses of $556 million, according to our estimates.[1] Disability compensation paid to injured service members (over and above that paid to uninjured service members) in our sample during this same period totaled $2.3 billion, 107 percent of estimated lost household earnings.

Because deployment-related injury and the associated DoD and VA compensation programs are unique, comparisons with other disability compensation systems must be made with appropriate caution.[2] Nevertheless, average replacement rates in workers' compensation programs (the disability insurance systems for civilian work-related injury managed by states) provide some context. In these programs, a common

---

[1] We compute aggregate household earnings loss by multiplying model parameter estimates by the number of observations of the corresponding injury, post-deployment year, and component cell and summing over components and post-deployment years. In interpreting the values in Table 7.1, it is important to recognize that estimated aggregate earnings losses are most certainly a lower limit on the actual aggregate earnings losses. Although our sample is large and comprehensive, it is likely to omit some fraction of those who were injured while deployed to Iraq and Afghanistan. Our aggregate analysis thus omits their income losses from the totals.

[2] For example, our analysis focuses on cash compensation available for injured veterans, but the VA and DoD provide a range of other programs, including vocational training and job placement, for injured veterans. These in-kind programs are not necessarily available through other disability compensation programs such as workers' compensation.

Table 7.1
Aggregate Earnings Losses Attributable to Injury, Net Disability Compensation, and Estimated Replacement Rates, by Injury Type: 2004–2010

Injury Type	Household Earnings Loss	Net Disability Compensation	Disability Compensation/ Earnings Loss (percentage)
Health worsened	557	363	65
Referred	1,048	937	89
Non-serious casualty	403	626	155
Serious casualty	89	205	230
Very serious casualty	63	173	275
All	2,160	2,304	107

NOTES: Estimates of aggregates computed by multiplying model parameter estimates by number of observations in corresponding injury, post-deployment year, and component cell and summing over components and post-deployment years. Net disability compensation is compensation paid above that paid to otherwise comparable uninjured service members. Aggregates employ estimates over all deployment cohorts and post-deployment years.

standard for benefit "adequacy" is replacement of two-thirds of gross wages (NASI, 2004). However, actual wage-replacement levels in workers' compensation systems are typically below this standard. Reville et al. (2001) found that two-year after-tax replacement rates for permanent-partial-disability workers' compensation claimants range from 38 to 60 percent across five states. A recent study of workers' compensation claims in California documents pre-tax five-year replacement rates that include the full spectrum of injured claimants in the 30- to 35-percent range (Seabury et al., 2011).[3] Studies of workers' compensation that compute replacement rates by severity of injury typically find higher replacement rates among the more seriously injured, as do we. Seabury et al. (2011), for example, report five-year pre-tax earnings replacement rates for low-, medium-, and high-severity claims in California of 12, 27, and 47 percent, respectively.

The fact that estimated replacement rates for combat-injured service members in our sample are substantially above 100 percent (see Table 6.9) may raise questions about the appropriateness of current levels of disability compensation. However, there are economic arguments for providing replacement rates above 100 percent for individuals with permanent or very serious injury. First, a large body of evidence suggests that individuals typically enjoy real wage gains as they grow older, particularly early

---

[3] These replacement rates do not take into account SSDI payments. However, unlike VA payments, workers' compensation payments and SSDI payments are offset so that the combined total cannot exceed 80 percent of pre-disability earnings.

in their careers. But disability payments, which are indexed for inflation, typically do not otherwise increase over time. Taking a lifecycle perspective, it may be logical to provide benefits above full replacement initially to account for the fact that those with permanent disability will not enjoy the earnings growth in later years that is expected for their uninjured peers. Economic theory also suggests that replacement rates above 100 percent can be justified for occupations in which calculated risk-taking is desirable (e.g., policing, firefighting, military service) (Seabury, 2002). For similar reasons, replacement rates above 100 percent might also serve to attract recruits to relatively risky military occupations. Additionally, if adaptation to serious or permanent injury entails additional out-of-pocket costs that are not faced by the uninjured,[4] it may be appropriate to compensate the injured at above 100 percent to offset these additional costs. Replacement rates above 100 percent might also serve to compensate seriously injured service members for reductions in quality of life that are unrelated to labor market earnings (e.g., pain and suffering, loss of consortium).

---

[4] For example, individuals with impaired mobility may require special vehicles or housing renovations to accommodate their mobility needs.

Specification Checks

This appendix presents full regression results corresponding to Tables 5.1 and 5.2 and the results of a variety of specification checks designed to examine the sensitivity of the results reported in Chapters Five and Six to alternative approaches to categorizing injury and specifying our empirical model.

Full Regression Results

Full regression results are given in Tables A.1 and A.2.

Table A.1
Estimated Effect of Injury on AC Household Labor Market Earnings, by Injury Type and Years Since Deployment: Full Regression Results (in 2010 dollars)

Variable	Year After Deployment			
	1	2	3	4
Health worsened	−1,414**	−2,229**	−2,391**	−2,693**
Referred	−1,993**	−3,952**	−4,340**	−4,651**
Non-serious casualty	−2,518**	−5,233**	−5,411**	−5,787**
Serious casualty	−3,977**	−10,466**	−11,447**	−11,943**
Very serious casualty	−7,680**	−18,328**	−22,292**	−22,555**
Death	−4,8067**	−51,112**	−50,272**	−50,395**
Age	−425**	−544**	−569**	−674**
Male	1,613**	4,166**	5,764**	7,010**
Missing gender	5,615**	6,751**	6,882**	7,963**
White	380**	−58	−480**	−816**
Black	558**	944**	920**	1,074**
Hispanic	−1,577**	−1,688**	−1,324**	−1,549**
Missing race	4,208**	4,001**	2,759**	2,306**
High school diploma	8,842**	10,223**	7,646**	6,928**
Some college	9,535**	11,075**	8,700**	8,516**

Table A.1—Continued

Variable	Year After Deployment			
	1	2	3	4
Bachelor's degree	10,464**	12,213**	10,441**	10,774**
Graduate degree	11,779**	14,375**	13,444**	14,703**
Missing education	8,461**	9,162**	6,583**	5,451**
AFQT	−56.309**	−52.337**	−59.789**	−46.005**
AFQT squared	0.221**	0.095	0.079	−0.056
Missing AFQT	−1,203**	−4,773**	−8,222**	−10,984**
Air Force	−179	−2,386**	−503**	638**
Navy	−559*	−2,017**	−1,318**	−1,437**
Marine Corps	971**	−2,591**	−2,773**	−1,300**
Pay grade: Senior enlisted (E5+)	1,275**	3,348**	5,234**	6,937**
Pay grade: Warrant Officer	9,075**	12,941**	16,038**	20,627**
Pay grade: Junior Officer (O1–O3)	2,289**	2,320**	3,420**	5,826**
Pay grade: Senior Officer (O4+)	6,070**	9,746**	13,655**	18,051**
Pay grade: Missing	26,630**	33,642**	32,901**	34,228**
Sought mental health counseling[a]	−2,614**	−4,126**	−4,617**	−5,505**
Missing mental health[a]	−334	185	−110	−449
Have a medical problem[a]	−452**	−1,186**	−1,439**	−1,418**
Currently on light duty[a]	−109	−1,149**	−1,294**	−1,801**
Self-reported health: Very good	−557**	−724**	−1,073**	−1,419**
Self-reported health: Good	−1,874**	−2,821**	−3,414**	−4,263**
Self-reported health: Fair	−4,646**	−6,180**	−6,688**	−7,327**
Self-reported health: Poor	−7,512**	−9,183**	−9,481**	−12,000**
Self-reported health: Missing	−484	−1,649*	−1,463*	−1,518
Deployment begin: 2002	−16,377*	−18,323*	−1,7118*	−3,212
Deployment begin: 2003	−23,951**	−26,089**	−24,016**	−10,396
Deployment begin: 2004	−28,086**	−31,163**	−29,870**	−17,691
Deployment begin: 2005	−32,309**	−35,316**	−34,894**	−22,346*
Deployment begin: 2006	−35,699**	−38,640**	−38,740**	−26,227*
Intercept	34,420**	38,181**	40,394**	29,122**
Number of observations	456,218	456,218"	456,218	456,218

NOTES: * denotes statistical significance at the 5-percent level; ** denotes statistical significance at the 1-percent level. Standard errors are robust to heteroskedasticity. Other model covariates include month and year deployment ends, dummies for state of residence, dummies for miiitary occupation specialty in both the year prior to deployment and while deployed. Ommited categorical variables include no injury, female, other race, no high school diploma, Army, junior enlisted (E-1–E-4), excellent self-reported health, and deployment begin: 2001.

[a] Measured prior to deployment.

Table A.2
Estimated Effect of Injury on RC Household Labor Market Earnings, by Injury Type and Years Since Deployment: Full Regression Results (in 2010 dollars)

Variable	Year After Deployment			
	1	2	3	4
Health worsened	−397*	−1,448**	−1,770**	−1,900**
Referred	−386**	−1,563**	−2,136**	−2,607**
Non-serious casualty	−126	−3,741**	−5,937**	−6,290**
Serious casualty	−1,123	−9,448**	−12,279**	−14,770**
Very serious casualty	−4,911*	−19,709**	−27,138**	−26,808**
Death	−43,677**	−47,979**	−51,155**	−51,929**
Age	−377**	−622**	−842**	−1,054**
Male	1,606**	2,670**	3,442**	3,743**
Missing gender	−3,194	−7,680	−2,236	−576
White	−36	−192	−464**	−410*
Black	702**	995**	973**	1,575**
Hispanic	430*	1,305**	1,513**	1,620**
Missing race	3,379**	3,716**	2,483*	1,897
High school diploma	8,743**	9,663**	10,045**	10,801**
Some college	9,227**	10,781**	11,405**	12,468**
Bachelor's degree	10,171**	11,466**	12,173**	13,440**
Graduate degre	9,613**	11,740**	12,813**	14,039**
Missing education	8,648**	9,627**	9,931**	10,341**
AFQT	−14.921	−13.803	−11.196	−23.883
AFQT squared	−0.057	0.056	0.264*	0.56**
Missing AFQT	−1,108**	−1,769**	−2,265**	−2,687**
Air Force	2,812**	1,623**	1,106**	1,202**
Navy	−244	784*	2,270**	2,672**
Marine Corps	−1,463**	−1,690**	−2,028**	−862*
Pay grade: Senior enlisted (E5+)	458**	1,175**	2,329**	4,066**
Pay grade: Warrant Officer	1,046	3,576**	6,900**	10,784**
Pay grade: Junior Officer (O1–O3)	4,988**	8,446**	13,329**	18,147**
Pay grade: Senior Officer (O4+)	6,068**	8,235**	11,681**	14,799**
Pay grade: Missing	18,328**	23,033**	25,813**	28,546**
Sought mental health counseling[a]	−1,239**	−1,985**	−2,258**	−2,764**
Missing mental health[a]	567	443	139	587
Have a medical problem[a]	−127	−208	−508*	−870**
Currently on light duty[a]	−60	−578*	−1,187**	−1,520**
Self-reported health: Very good	−896**	−1,186**	−1,538**	−1,933**
Self-reported health: Good	−1,779**	−2,529**	−3,120**	−3,777**

Table A.2—Continued

Variable	Year After Deployment			
	1	2	3	4
Self-reported health: Fair	−2,861**	−4,198**	−4,536**	−5,382**
Self-reported health: Poor	−3,704*	−3,236	−3,697	−5,363*
Self-reported health: Missing	−1,167*	−1,444*	−1,539*	−2,443**
Deployment begin: 2002	1,979	1,716	275	2,807
Deployment begin: 2003	−3,169	−5,321*	−6,332	−3,956
Deployment begin: 2004	−6,935**	−11,475**	−12,039**	−10,954**
Deployment begin: 2005	−11,561**	−16,691**	−17,643**	−15,927**
Deployment begin: 2006	−15,803**	−20,637**	−22,101**	−20,403**
Intercept	10,982**	18,091**	23,906**	26,559**
Number of observations	236,580	236,580	236,580	236,580

NOTES: * denotes statistical significance at the 5-percent level; ** denotes statistical significance at the 1-percent level. Standard errors are robust to heteroskedasticity. Other model covariates include month and year deployment ends, dummies for state of residence, dummies for military occupation specialty in both the year prior to deployment and while deployed. Omitted categorical variables include no injury, female, other race, no high school diploma, Army, junior enlisted (E-1–E-4), excellent self-reported health, and deployment begin: 2001.

a Measured prior to deployment.

Chapter Five Specification Checks

We were able to examine at least four post-deployment years for all individuals in our sample, as described in Chapter Five. We also have additional post-deployment earnings data for individuals who ended deployments prior to 2006. Tables A.3 and A.4 present estimates of the impact of injury on household earnings up to seven years following deployment. In general, estimated effects on earnings do not vary significantly between years 4 and 7, which suggests that earnings losses in the injured population stabilize by year 4. Because the sample changes for earnings beyond year 4 so that we cannot distinguish between time and cohort effects, we re-estimated these specifications focusing only on individuals who ended their deployment in 2003 (see Tables A.5 and A.6). This substantially reduces the number of observations available for estimating the impact of injury, but it allows us to assess patterns in earnings loss for years 1 through 7 over a consistently defined population. Results for this balanced sample also imply that earnings losses are relatively stable after year 4. There is evidence that earnings losses increase somewhat between years 4 and 7 among very serious casualties, but this increase is only suggestive, as the earnings differences across these years are not statistically significant.

Table A.3
Estimated Effect of Injury on AC Household Labor Market Earnings, by Injury Type and Years Since Deployment: Unbalanced Panel (in 2010 dollars)

Year After Deployment	Injury Type				
	Health Worsened	Referred	Non-Serious Casualty	Serious Casualty	Very Serious Casualty
1	−1,414** (134)	−1,993** (142)	−2,518** (202)	−3,977** (603)	−7,680** (1,032)
2	−2,229** (163)	−3,952** (173)	−5,233** (246)	−10,466** (756)	−18,328** (1,351)
3	−2,391** (175)	−4,340** (185)	−5,411** (265)	−11,447** (829)	−22,292** (1,419)
4	−2,693** (191)	−4,651** (200)	−5,787** (287)	−11,943** (893)	−22,555** (1,476)
5	−2,623** (236)	−4,479** (242)	−4,868** (390)	−13,102** (1,099)	−23,105** (1,854)
6	−2,241** (309)	−4,429** (322)	−5,722** (600)	−12,408** (1,335)	−21,288** (2,428)
7	−1,897** (541)	−4,379** (578)	−7,831** (1,795)	−8,158 (4,384)	−20,807** (4,961)

NOTES: Authors' calculations from an unbalanced panel of 456,218 AC service members in years 1–4; 327,353 in year 5; 196,419 in year 6; and 64,685 in year 7. Heteroskedasticity-robust standard errors are in parentheses; * denotes statistical significance at the 5-percent level, ** denotes statistical significance at the 1-percent level.

Table A.4
Estimated Effect of Injury on RC Household Labor Market Earnings, by Injury Type and Years Since Deployment: Unbalanced Panel (in 2010 dollars)

Year After Deployment	Injury Type				
	Health Worsened	Referred	Non-Serious Casualty	Serious Casualty	Very Serious Casualty
1	−397* (157)	−386** (131)	−126 (318)	−1,123 (1,191)	−4,911* (2,129)
2	−1,448** (183)	−1,563** (153)	−3,741** (372)	−9,448** (1,394)	−19,709** (2,377)
3	−1,770** (207)	−2,136** (173)	−5,937** (430)	−12,279** (1,560)	−27,138** (2,519)
4	−1,900** (228)	−2,607** (191)	−6,290** (478)	−14,770** (1,707)	−26,808** (2,741)
5	−1,836** (277)	−2,907** (227)	−5,717** (610)	−14,074** (2,101)	−30,361** (3,521)
6	−1,691** (410)	−2,628** (339)	−4,395** (1,181)	−13,496** (3,058)	−35,477** (4,486)
7	−1,739* (743)	−3,568** (696)	−5,862* (2,918)	−14,110* (6,095)	−29,308** (8,881)

NOTES: Authors' calculations from an unbalanced panel of 236,580 RC service members in years 1–4, 185,305 in year 5, 88,702 in year 6, and 26,793 in year 7. Heteroskedasticity-robust standard errors are in parentheses; * denotes statistical significance at the 5-percent level, ** denotes statistical significance at the 1-percent level.

Table A.5
Estimated Effect of Injury on AC Household Labor Market Earnings, by Injury Type and Years Since Deployment: Balanced Panel (in 2010 dollars)

Year After Deployment	Injury Type				
	Health Worsened	Referred	Non-Serious Casualty	Serious Casualty	Very Serious Casualty
1	−431 (289)	−123 (321)	1,150 (1,024)	−2,460 (2,324)	−1,953 (3,220)
2	−1,850** (372)	−3,140** (416)	−3,818** (1,418)	−11,382** (3,298)	−11,370* (4,437)
3	−2,367** (401)	−3,958** (446)	−8,039** (1,393)	−14,034** (3,491)	−14,044** (4,347)
4	−1,886** (440)	−3,690** (478)	−9,194** (1,491)	−14,017** (3,907)	−13,598** (5,015)
5	−1,527** (459)	−3,777** (507)	−7,728** (1,664)	−13,754** (3,950)	−18,947** (4,813)
6	−1,818** (508)	−4,188** (550)	−7,897** (1,798)	−11,484** (3,901)	−22,184** (4,962)
7	−1,897** (541)	−4,379** (578)	−7,831** (1,795)	−8,158 (4,384)	−20,807** (4,961)

NOTES: Authors' calculations from a balanced sample of 64,685 AC service members ending deployment in 2003. Heteroskedasticity-robust standard errors are in parentheses.; * denotes statistical significance at the 5-percent level; ** denotes statistical significance at the 1-percent level.

Table A.6
Estimated Effect of Injury on RC Household Labor Market Earnings, by Injury Type and Years Since Deployment: Balanced Panel (in 2010 dollars)

Year After Deployment	Injury Type				
	Health Worsened	Referred	Non-Serious Casualty	Serious Casualty	Very Serious Casualty
1	35 (414)	944* (394)	4,929** (1,597)	2,990 (3,660)	−7,050 (9,013)
2	−1,761** (479)	−1,911** (461)	−6,433** (1,562)	−9,407* (4,052)	−18,280 (10,726)
3	−1,365* (533)	−1,946** (519)	−6,814** (1,994)	−9,264* (4,339)	−20,213 (11,614)
4	−1,809** (585)	−2,860** (556)	−7,655** (2,277)	−15,462** (4,330)	−22,346 (12,795)
5	−1,632* (638)	−3,399** (600)	−8,406** (2,646)	−12,130** (3,524)	−25,941* (11,910)
6	−2,030** (700)	−3,800** (651)	−9,298** (2,777)	−11,150* (4,769)	−30,136** (10,473)
7	−1,739* (743)	−3,568** (696)	−5,862* (2,918)	−14,110* (6,095)	−29,308** (8,881)

NOTES: Authors' calculations from a balanced sample of 26,793 RC serviceme mbers ending deployment in 2003. Heteroskedasticity-robust standard errors are in parentheses; * denotes statistical significance at the 5-percent level; ** denotes statistical significance at the 1-percent level.

How sensitive are these results to our particular method for categorizing injury? One potential concern is that the self-reported health data from the PDHA may be less reliable than data from the official casualty reporting system. Tables A.7 and A.8 present specifications that use only information contained in DMDC's Casualty File,

Table A.7
Estimated Effect of Injury on AC Household Labor Market Earnings, by Injury Type and Years Since Deployment (in 2010 dollars)

Year After Deployment	Injury Type		
	Non-Serious Casualty	Serious Casualty	Very Serious Casualty
1	−2,263**	−3,759**	−7,444**
	(201)	(602)	(1,032)
2	−4,772**	−10,076**	−17,904**
	(245)	(755)	(1,350)
3	−4,909**	−11,023**	−21,830**
	(264)	(828)	(1,418)
4	−5,239**	−11,479**	−22,050**
	(287)	(892)	(1,475)

NOTES: Authors' calculations from a balanced sample of 456,218 AC service members. Uninjured group includes self-reported and referrals. Heteroskedasticity-robust standard errors are in parentheses; * denotes statistical significance at the 5-percent level; ** denotes statistical significance at the 1-percent level.

Table A.8
Estimated Effect of Injury on RC Household Labor Market Earnings, by Injury Type and Years Since Deployment (in 2010 dollars)

Year After Deployment	Injury Type		
	Non-Serious Casualty	Serious Casualty	Very Serious Casualty
1	−29	−1,032	−4,822*
	(317)	(1,191)	(2,129)
2	−3,365**	−9,094**	−19,367**
	(371)	(1,394)	(2,374)
3	−5,443**	−11,817**	−26,691**
	(429)	(1,560)	(2,514)
4	−5,712**	−14,232**	−26,288**
	(477)	(1,706)	(2,735)

NOTES: Authors' calculations from a balanced sample of 236,580 RC service members. Uninjured group includes self-reported and referrals. Heteroskedasticity-robust standard errors are in parentheses; * denotes statistical significance at the 5-percent level; ** denotes statistical significance at the 1-percent level.

categorizing injuries as non-serious, serious, or very serious and coding everyone who does not appear in the Casualty File as uninjured. Using this injury categorization yields very similar results to the baseline results presented in Tables 5.1 and 5.2.

Using the casualty data, we can also examine the sensitivity of our results to the inclusion or exclusion of individuals who were subsequently redeployed and sustained injury after the period covered by our sample. At a conceptual level, there are advantages to both excluding and including such individuals from the analysis. The main rationale for including service members who later sustain injuries, as we do in our main analysis, is that the proper counterfactual for the earnings of the injured is whatever they would have earned had they not been injured during the deployment in question. Potential future scenarios for the uninjured include the possibility of additional deployment and subsequent injury, so the estimates should arguably incorporate such possibilities. An argument for excluding those with future injuries, however, is that if a goal of compensation policy is to allow injured individuals to enjoy economic outcomes similar to those of service members with good health, the most appropriate comparison is between those who are injured and those who are not. In this view, failing to exclude those with subsequent injuries would inappropriately contaminate the comparison group with individuals who are in less-than-perfect health.

In Tables A.9 and A.10 we reestimate specifications incorporating injury information from the Casualty File only, but excluding the individuals who appear in the file after 2006.[1] The actual number of control personnel from our primary sample who were recorded as casualties after 2006 is small, so it is unsurprising that this restriction has little effect on our estimates or conclusions. Thus, as a practical matter, this distinction appears to be unimportant for our analysis. We note, however, that in an analysis that incorporated richer data on health status after 2006 than simple casualty indicators, one might observe larger differences between the results obtained using the full set of controls rather than only the uninjured.[2]

Many prior studies of disability compensation use disability ratings rather than injury categories as measures of injury. Tables A.11–A.14 present estimates using alternative injury categorizations based on DoD disability ratings. The results for household labor market earnings are qualitatively similar to those based on DMDC's categorization in the Casualty File.[3]

---

[1] There are 4,680 such individuals in the AC and 908 in the RC.

[2] PDHA data were available only through mid-2007, so we could not use them to look at health in later years.

[3] For other earnings outcomes such as spousal earnings and military and civilian earnings, we observe similar patterns to those we obtained using alternative injury categorizations, balanced samples, and samples restricted to the never-injured.

Table A.9
Estimated Effect of Injury on AC Household Labor Market Earnings, by Injury Type and Years Since Deployment, Excluding Casualties After 2006 (in 2010 dollars)

Year After Deployment	Injury Type		
	Non-Serious Casualty	Serious Casualty	Very Serious Casualty
1	−2,093**	−3,615**	−7,286**
	(201)	(603)	(1,032)
2	−4,555**	−9,856**	−17,701**
	(245)	(755)	(1,350)
3	−4,772**	−10,856**	−21,695**
	(264)	(828)	(1,418)
4	−5,176**	−11,376**	−21,988**
	(287)	(892)	(1,475)

NOTES: Authors' calculations from a balanced sample of 451,538 AC service members who do not appear in the Casualty File after 2006. Uninjured group includes self-reported and referrals. Heteroskedasticity-robust standard errors are in parentheses; *denotes statistical significance at the 5-percent level; ** denotes statistical significance at the 1-percent level.

Table A.10
Estimated Effect of Injury on RC Household Labor Market Earnings, by Injury Type and Years Since Deployment, Excluding Casualties After 2006 (in 2010 dollars)

Year After Deployment	Injury Type		
	Non-Serious Casualty	Serious Casualty	Very Serious Casualty
1	14	−997	−4,776*
	(317)	(1,192)	(2,129)
2	−3,310**	−9,056**	−19,312**
	(371)	(1,393)	(2,373)
3	−5,410**	−11,787**	−26,652**
	(429)	(1,559)	(2,513)
4	−5,696**	−14,211**	−26,264**
	(477)	(1,706)	(2,733)

NOTES: Authors' calculations from a balanced sample of 235,672 RC service members who do not appear in the Casualty File after 2006. Uninjured group includes self-reported and referrals. Heteroskedasticity-robust standard errors are in parentheses; * denotes statistical significance at the 5-percent level; ** denotes statistical significance at the 1-percent level.

Table A.11

Estimated Effect of Injury on AC Household Labor Market Earnings, by Injury Type and Years Since Deployment: Alternative Injury Categorization (in 2010 dollars)

Year After Deployment	Health Worsened	Referred	Disability Rating (percent)			
			0	10–40	50–70	80–100
1	−1,415**	−1,994**	−2,302**	−5,712**	−3,238**	−9,451**
	(134)	(142)	(207)	(623)	(692)	(1,063)
2	−2,232**	−3,958**	−3,931**	−18,194**	−14,934**	−23,705**
	(163)	(173)	(249)	(779)	(908)	(1,229)
3	−2,395**	−4,347**	−3,261**	−22,582**	−22,182**	−30,994**
	(175)	(185)	(264)	(883)	(989)	(1,228)
4	−2,697**	−4,659**	−3,053**	−24,552**	−26,736**	−35,910**
	(191)	(200)	(286)	(891)	(1,006)	(1,283)

NOTES: Heteroskedasticity-robust standard errors are in parentheses; * denotes statistical significance at the 5-percent level; ** denotes statistical significance at the 1-percent level.

Table A.12

Estimated Effect of Injury on RC Household Labor Market Earnings, by Injury Type and Years Since Deployment: Alternative Injury Categorization (in 2010 dollars)

Year After Deployment	Health Worsened	Referred	Disability Rating (percent)			
			0	10–40	50–70	80–100
1	−396*	−386**	−799*	4,412**	3,045*	−1123
	(157)	(131)	(321)	(1,406)	(1,354)	(1,997)
2	−1,449**	−1,567**	−3,191**	−9,221**	−12,112**	−17,857**
	(183)	(153)	(376)	(1,644)	(1,464)	(2,360)
3	−1,773**	−2,143**	−4,107**	−17,743**	−23,862**	−30,749**
	(207)	(173)	(427)	(1,767)	(1,622)	(2,586)
4	−1,904**	−2,615**	−3,912**	−21,300**	−26,239**	−40,001**
	(228)	(191)	(474)	(1,837)	(1,792)	(2,592)

NOTES: Heteroskedasticity-robust standard errors are in parentheses; * denotes statistical significance at the 5-percent level; ** denotes statistical significance at the 1-percent level.

Table A.13
Estimated Effect of Injury on AC Household Labor Market
Earnings, by Injury Type and Years Since Deployment:
Alternative Injury Categorization, Excluding Casualties After
2006 (in 2010 dollars)

Year After Deployment	Disability Rating (percent)			
	0	10–40	50–70	80–100
1	−2,051**	−5,470**	−2,980**	−9,189**
	(206)	(623)	(692)	(1,063)
2	−3,477**	−17,758**	−14,467**	−23,230**
	(248)	(779)	(908)	(1,229)
3	−2,767**	−22,108**	−21,673**	−30,477**
	(264)	(882)	(989)	(1,228)
4	−2,513**	−24,034**	−26,181**	−35,345**
	(285)	(890)	(1,005)	(1,283)

NOTES: Authors' calculations from a balanced sample of 451,538
AC service members who do not appear in the Casualty File
after 2006. Uninjured group includes self-reported and referrals.
Heteroskedasticity-robust standard errors are in parentheses;
* denotes statistical significance at the 5-percent level; ** denotes
statistical significance at the 1-percent level.

Table A.14
Estimated Effect of Injury on RC Household Labor Market
Earnings, by Injury Type and Years Since Deployment:
Alternative Injury Categorization, Excluding Casualties After
2006 (in 2010 dollars)

Year After Deployment	Disability Rating (percent)			
	0	10–40	50–70	80–100
1	−703*	4,511**	3,147*	−1,025
	(320)	(1,406)	(1,354)	(1,996)
2	−2,819**	−8,836**	−11,715**	−17,475**
	(375)	(1,645)	(1,464)	(2,359)
3	−3,618**	−17,238**	−23,340**	−30,248**
	(426)	(1,767)	(1,622)	(2,582)
4	−3,340**	−20,710**	−25,629**	−39,415**
	(472)	(1,838)	(1,791)	(2,588)

NOTES: Authors' calculations from a balanced sample of 235,672
RC service members who do not appear in the Casualty File after
2006. Uninjured group includes self-reported and referrals.
Heteroskedasticity-robust standard errors are in parentheses;
* denotes statistical significance at the 5-percent level; ** denotes
statistical significance at the 1-percent level.

Chapter Six Specification Checks

Like Chapter Five, Chapter Six focuses on the first four years after deployment. Here, we explore what happens to household income in later years under our first set of alternative specifications. Tables A.15 and A.16 report estimated effects of injury on household income, including DoD and VA retirement and disability payments, CRSC, SSDI, and TSGLI (comparable to Tables 6.7 and 6.8) for years 1 through 7 after deployment, using all available observations in each year. Sample sizes are constant across years 1 through 4, and the results for those years are identical to those reported in Tables 6.7 and 6.8.

The estimated effects of injury on household income in years 5 through 7 are generally similar to those for year 4. For all but the most severe injury groups (very serious casualties for AC and serious and very serious casualties for RC), the estimated effects are more positive after year 4. For AC members with self-reported health changes or referrals—the only injury groups with significant declines in household income in year 4—the estimates decrease in years 5 and 6 and are small (under $500) and statistically insignificant in year 7.

Table A.15
Estimated Effect of Injury on AC Household Income, by Injury Type and Years Since Deployment: Unbalanced Panel (in 2010 dollars)

Year After Deployment	Injury Type				
	Health Worsened	Referred	Non-Serious Casualty	Serious Casualty	Very Serious Casualty
1	−1,067** (131)	−1,402** (137)	3,717** (291)	24,824** (1,482)	74,144** (3,387)
2	−1,525** (156)	−2,397** (163)	627* (270)	14,746** (1,356)	31,748** (2,603)
3	−1,318** (167)	−2,086** (173)	853** (258)	6,972** (972)	2,0381** (1,794)
4	−1,354** (181)	−1,863** (186)	1,102** (269)	6,381** (894)	19,976** (1,540)
5	−1,151** (223)	−1,457** (227)	2,259** (369)	7,467** (1,164)	17,611** (1,961)
6	−677* (293)	−988** (302)	3,066** (559)	8,774** (1,366)	15,625** (2,523)
7	−102 (514)	−403 (545)	3,156 (1,806)	13,403** (3,987)	13,454* (5,774)

NOTES: Authors' calculations from an unbalanced panel of 456,218 AC service members in years 1-4, 327,353 service members in year 5, 196,419 service members in year 6, and 64,685 service members in year 7. Heteroskedasticity-robust standard errors are in parentheses; * denotes statistical significance at the 5-percent level; ** denotes statistical significance at the 1-percent level.

Table A.16
Estimated Effect of Injury on RC Household Income, by Injury Type and Years
Since Deployment: Unbalanced Panel (in 2010 dollars)

Year After Deployment	Health Worsened	Referred	Non-Serious Casualty	Serious Casualty	Very Serious Casualty
			Injury Type		
1	136 (156)	485** (130)	6,697** (475)	28,357** (2,810)	88,049** (7,419)
2	−312 (179)	507** (150)	3,574** (416)	24,021** (3,031)	42,089** (5,239)
3	−73 (201)	1,001** (167)	3,662** (432)	11,356** (1,750)	26,583** (4,155)
4	166 (220)	1,301** (182)	4,550** (461)	12,337** (1,954)	27,780** (3,734)
5	417 (266)	1,441** (215)	5,412** (589)	14,736** (2,177)	22,726** (4,185)
6	672 (396)	1,785** (322)	9,,473** (1153)	17,009** (3,470)	18,958** (5,979)
7	694 (718)	1,674* (660)	10,520** (2,887)	8,112 (5,286)	45,603** (15,621)

NOTES: Authors' calculations from an unbalanced panel of 236,580 RC service members in years 1–4, 185,305 service members in year 5, 88,702 service members in year 6, and 26,793 service members in year 7. Heteroskedasticity-robust standard errors are in parentheses; * denotes statistical significance at the 5-percent level; ** denotes statistical significance at the 1-percent level.

These results suggest that all injury groups are fully compensated in the longer term. However, because these estimates are based on all the available observations, not all of the households are present in all seven years. Because the panel is not balanced over time, the year-to-year changes in the estimates could in part reflect the changing composition of the sample as it is limited to earlier and earlier deployments. We test this hypothesis by estimating the effects from year 1 through 7 on a balanced sample of households with deployments ending in 2003.

The results, reported in Appendix Tables A.17 and A.18, indicate that compositional changes are indeed part of the explanation for the increasing effect of injury on household income after year 4. In particular, AC members with self-reported injuries and referrals in the balanced sample have smaller (and less statistically significant) income losses in year 4 than the same group in the unbalanced sample. Nevertheless, the income losses decrease after year 4 for these groups in the balanced panel as well, which suggests that sample composition is not solely to blame.

Table A.17
Estimated Effect of Injury on AC Household Income, by Injury Type and Years Since Deployment: Balanced Panel (in 2010 dollars)

Year After Deployment	Injury Type				
	Health Worsened	Referred	Non-Serious Casualty	Serious Casualty	Very Serious Casualty
1	−193 (283)	418 (311)	2,531* (1,009)	2,827 (2,408)	9,971** (3,505)
2	−1,060** (359)	−1,474** (389)	953 (1,454)	7,311 (4,533)	16,651** (6,099)
3	−1,283** (387)	−1,640** (414)	4,569* (1,874)	22,212** (6,104)	48,580** (11,874)
4	−634 (419)	−892* (446)	−998 (1,467)	5,133 (4,057)	15,977** (4,416)
5	−81 (437)	−648 (477)	2,349 (1,691)	4,367 (3,723)	9,646* (4,482)
6	−236 (483)	−463 (520)	3,537* (17,90)	10,660** (4,087)	12,186* (6,079)
7	−102 (514)	−403 (545)	3,156 (1,806)	13,403** (3,987)	13,454* (5,774)

NOTES: Authors' calculations from a balanced sample of 64,685 AC service members ending deployment in 2003. Heteroskedasticity-robust standard errors are in parentheses; * denotes statistical significance at the 5-percent level; ** denotes statistical significance at the 1-percent level.

Table A.18
Estimated Effect of Injury on RC Household Income, by Injury Type and Years Since Deployment: Balanced Panel (in 2010 dollars)

Year After Deployment	Injury Type				
	Health Worsened	Referred	Non-Serious Casualty	Serious Casualty	Very Serious Casualty
1	374 (416)	1,526** (392)	8,096** (1,764)	5,188 (3,536)	36,075* (14,955)
2	−736 (473)	47 (446)	4,438* (1,915)	10,101 (8,149)	76,445** (24,247)
3	185 (532)	992* (500)	8,997** (2,286)	8,044 (5,730)	131,260** (42,869)
4	26 (571)	812 (527)	8,359** (2,236)	2,736 (5,079)	48,811** (15,070)
5	276 (618)	977 (569)	6,552* (2,557)	5,565 (3,914)	43,147** (14,303)
6	229 (677)	1,301* (618)	9,015** (2,954)	8,811* (3,985)	44,932** (16,963)
7	694 (718)	1,674* (660)	10,520** (2,887)	8,112 (5,286)	45,603** (15,621)

NOTES: Authors' calculations from a balanced sample of 26,793 RC service members ending deployment in 2003. Heteroskedasticity-robust standard errors are in parentheses; * denotes statistical significance at the 5-percent level; ** denotes statistical significance at the 1-percent level.

As in Chapter Five, a second set of alternative specifications explores the sensitivity of our main results to changes in how we define injury and whether we exclude individuals who appear in the Casualty File after 2006. These results are reported in Tables A.19 through A.26. Results obtained from these alternative specifications are broadly consistent with the baseline results reported in Tables 6.7 and 6.8.

Table A.19
Estimated Effect of Injury on AC Household Income, by Injury Type and Years Since Deployment (in 2010 dollars)

Year After Deployment	Injury Type		
	Non-Serious Casualty	Serious Casualty	Very Serious Casualty
1	3,902**	24,982**	74,315**
	(290)	(1,482)	(3,387)
2	920**	14,995**	32,018**
	(269)	(1,356)	(2,603)
3	1,107**	7,188**	20,616**
	(258)	(972)	(1,794)
4	1,343**	6,587**	20,198**
	(268)	(893)	(1,540)

NOTES: Authors' calculations from a balanced sample of 456,218 AC service members. Uninjured group includes self-reported and referrals. Heteroskedasticity-robust standard errors are in parentheses; * denotes statistical significance at the 5-percent level; ** denotes statistical significance at the 1-percent level.

Table A.20
Estimated Effect of Injury on RC Household Income, by Injury Type and Years Since Deployment (in 2010 dollars)

Year After Deployment	Injury Type		
	Non-Serious Casualty	Serious Casualty	Very Serious Casualty
1	6,610**	28,279**	87,974**
	(474)	(2,810)	(7,419)
2	3,528**	23,985**	42,056**
	(415)	(3,031)	(5,239)
3	3,518**	11,231**	26,463**
	(431)	(1,749)	(4,156)
4	4,337**	12,147**	27,599**
	(460)	(1,953)	(3,735)

NOTES: Authors' calculations from a balanced sample of 236,580 RC service members. Uninjured group includes self-reported and referrals. Heteroskedasticity-robust standard errors are in parentheses; * denotes statistical significance at the 5-percent level; ** denotes statistical significance at the 1-percent level.

Table A.21
Estimated Effect of Injury on AC Household Income, by Injury Type and Years Since Deployment, Excluding Casualties After 2006 (in 2010 dollars)

Year After Deployment	Injury Type		
	Non-Serious Casualty	Serious Casualty	Very Serious Casualty
1	4,089**	25,168**	74,490**
	(291)	(1,483)	(3,388)
2	1,222**	15,298**	32,294**
	(269)	(1,357)	(2,603)
3	1,349**	7,453**	20,847**
	(258)	(972)	(1,795)
4	1,533**	6,814**	20,382**
	(268)	(893)	(1,541)

NOTES: Authors' calculations from a balanced sample of 451,538 AC service members who do not appear in the Casualty File after 2006. Uninjured group includes self-reported and referrals. Heteroskedasticity-robust standard errors are in parentheses; * denotes statistical significance at the 5-percent level; ** denotes statistical significance at the 1-percent level.

Table A.22
Estimated Effect of Injury on RC Household Income, by Injury Type and Years Since Deployment, Excluding Casualties After 2006 (in 2010 dollars)

Year After Deployment	Injury Type		
	Non-Serious Casualty	Serious Casualty	Very Serious Casualty
1	6,656**	28,315**	88,025**
	(474)	(2,810)	(7,420)
2	3,595**	24,031**	42,124**
	(415)	(3,031)	(5,238)
3	3,585**	11,277**	26,535**
	(431)	(1,750)	(4,155)
4	4,395**	12,195**	27,670**
	(460)	(1,953)	(3,734)

NOTES: Authors' calculations from a balanced sample of 235,672 RC service members who do not appear in the Casualty File after 2006. Uninjured group includes self-reported and referrals. Heteroskedasticity-robust standard errors are in parentheses; * denotes statistical significance at the 5-percent level; ** denotes statistical significance at the 1-percent level.

Table A.23
Estimated Effect of Injury on AC Household Income, by Injury Type and
Years Since Deployment, Alternative Injury Categorization
(in 2010 dollars)

Year After Deployment	Health Worsened	Referred	Disability Rating (percent)			
			0	10–40	50–70	80–100
1	–1,052**	–1,373**	1,188**	22,621**	36,239**	95,475**
	(131)	(137)	(255)	(1,522)	(1,929)	(3,356)
2	–1,517**	–2,381**	–467	9,107**	19,997**	43,917**
	(156)	(163)	(266)	(1,306)	(1,595)	(2,662)
3	–1,313**	–2,077**	–63	3,979**	10,914**	33,596**
	(167)	(173)	(256)	(1,073)	(1,132)	(1,829)
4	–1,350**	–1,854**	514	2,260*	9,292**	29,785**
	(181)	(186)	(272)	(967)	(980)	(1,550)

NOTES: Heteroskedasticity-robust standard errors are in parentheses; * denotes
statistical significance at the 5-percent level; ** denotes statistical significance at
the 1-percent level.

Table A.24
Estimated Effect of Injury on RC Household Income, by Injury Type and
Years Since Deployment, Alternative Injury Categorization
(in 2010 dollars)

Year After Deployment	Health Worsened	Referred	Disability Rating (percent)			
			0	10–40	50–70	80–100
1	144	506**	3,122**	32,294**	48,990**	86,295**
	(156)	(130)	(395)	(2,774)	(3,514)	(6,085)
2	–308	520**	1,757**	21,790**	25,346**	52,813**
	(179)	(150)	(412)	(2,374)	(2,501)	(4,898)
3	–70	1,007**	1,996**	16,814**	16,463**	35,116**
	(201)	(167)	(425)	(1,943)	(1,830)	(3,688)
4	170	1,308**	2,969**	17,021**	21,025**	29,215**
	(220)	(182)	(460)	(2,128)	(1,937)	(3,457)

NOTES: Heteroskedasticity-robust standard errors are in parentheses; * denotes
statistical significance at the 5-percent level; ** denotes statistical significance at
the 1-percent level.

Table A.25
Estimated Effect of Injury on AC Household Income, by Injury Type and Years Since Deployment, Alternative Injury Categorization, Excluding Casualties After 2006 (in 2010 dollars)

Year After Deployment	Disability Rating (percent)			
	0	10–40	50–70	80–100
1	1,367**	22,793**	36,423**	95,662**
	(255)	(1,522)	(1,929)	(3,356)
2	–181	9,382**	20,292**	44,217**
	(265)	(1,305)	(1,594)	(2,662)
3	186	4,218**	11,170**	33,856**
	(256)	(1,073)	(1,131)	(1,829)
4	750**	2,488*	9,535**	30,032**
	(272)	(967)	(980)	(1,550)

NOTES: Authors' calculations from a balanced sample of 451,538 AC service members who do not appear in the Casualty File after 2006. Uninjured group includes self-reported and referrals. Heteroskedasticity-robust standard errors are in parentheses; * denotes statistical significance at the 5-percent level; ** denotes statistical significance at the 1-percent level.

Table A.26
Estimated Effect of Injury on RC Household Income, by Injury Type and Years Since Deployment, Alternative Injury Categorization, Excluding Casualties After 2006 (in 2010 dollars)

Year After Deployment	Disability Rating (percent)			
	0	10–40	50–70	80–100
1	3,033**	32,203**	48,895**	86,204**
	(394)	(2,773)	(3,514)	(6,086)
2	1,709**	21,744**	25,295**	52,764**
	(412)	(2,374)	(2,501)	(4,898)
3	1,853**	16,669**	16,310**	34,969**
	(424)	(1,942)	(1,829)	(3,689)
4	2,758**	16,807**	20,800**	28,999**
	(459)	(2,127)	(1,936)	(3,458)

NOTES: Authors' calculations from a balanced sample of 235,672 RC service members who do not appear in the Casualty File after 2006. Uninjured group includes self-reported and referrals. Heteroskedasticity-robust standard errors are in parentheses; * denotes statistical significance at the 5-percent level; ** denotes statistical significance at the 1-percent level.

Distribution of Estimated Replacement Rates

Table 6.9 reports estimated mean replacement rates by component, injury type, and year since deployment. This appendix provides further detail on the full distribution of estimated replacement rates within these groups.

As described in Chapter Six, we define *replacement rate* as the ratio of actual household income including disability payments to expected household income in the absence of injury. Thus, if a service member (and spouse) earned $50,000 including disability payments in a given post-deployment year but would have earned $55,000 had he or she not been injured, the estimated replacement rate for that individual would be 91 percent (i.e., $50,000/$55,000). We computed expected household income for each service member in each post-deployment year by adding the predicted increase in household income from the regression model described in Chapter Four to actual household income in the pre-deployment year, ignoring the parameter estimates for injury. Expected household income is the household income our regression model predicts a service member would have earned in a given post-deployment year had he or she not been injured. A decline in household income relative to expected household income results in a replacement rate of less than 100 percent; an increase results in a replacement rate of more than 100 percent.

Table B.1 shows the full distribution of estimated replacement rates, including TSGLI income, by injury type and year since deployment for AC members. We compute estimated replacement rates for the uninjured as well as the injured, because both experience idiosyncratic income shocks (as proxied by the error term in our regression model) leading to deviations of actual household income from expected household income that are independent of injury. Thus, some uninjured service members will experience replacement rates of less than 100 percent, and others will experience replacement rates of more than 100 percent for reasons unrelated to injury. However, the mean replacement rate for the uninjured is close to 100 percent, and the median replacement rate is exactly 100 percent. The tables then show, as we would expect, that the mean and median replacement rates are significantly greater than 100 percent for seriously and very seriously injured service members: 58 percent and 63 percent of seriously and very seriously injured service members, respectively, have a replacement rate of more than 100 percent in year 4. Seriously and very seriously injured service members are 16 and 46 percent less likely than the uninjured to have replacement rates of less than 100 percent in year 4. Table B.2 reports replacement rates for the AC, excluding TSGLI. Tables B.3 and B.4 report replacement rates, including and excluding TSGLI, for the RC. Figures B.1 and B.2 are histograms of estimated replacement rates in year 4 including TSGLI income for the AC and RC, respectively.

Table B.1
Distribution of Estimated Replacement Rates, Including TSGLI Income, by Injury Type and Years Since Deployment: AC

Injury Type/ Years Since Deployment	Replacement Rate (percent)													Mean Rep. Rate
	0–25	25–50	50–75	75–100	100–125	125–150	150–175	175–200	200–225	225–250	250–275	275–300	300+	
Uninjured														
1	0.04	0.05	0.11	0.29	0.27	0.12	0.06	0.03	0.01	0.01	0.00	0.00	0.00	1.04
2	0.06	0.07	0.12	0.25	0.24	0.13	0.06	0.03	0.02	0.01	0.01	0.00	0.01	1.03
3	0.08	0.07	0.12	0.23	0.23	0.13	0.07	0.03	0.02	0.01	0.01	0.00	0.01	1.03
4	0.10	0.07	0.12	0.21	0.22	0.13	0.07	0.04	0.02	0.01	0.01	0.00	0.01	1.02
Self-reported														
1	0.05	0.07	0.12	0.27	0.26	0.12	0.06	0.02	0.01	0.01	0.00	0.00	0.00	1.01
2	0.08	0.08	0.13	0.23	0.23	0.12	0.06	0.03	0.02	0.01	0.01	0.00	0.01	1.00
3	0.10	0.08	0.12	0.22	0.22	0.12	0.06	0.03	0.02	0.01	0.01	0.00	0.01	0.99
4	0.11	0.09	0.12	0.20	0.21	0.12	0.07	0.03	0.02	0.01	0.01	0.00	0.01	0.99
Referred														
1	0.06	0.07	0.12	0.27	0.25	0.12	0.05	0.03	0.01	0.01	0.00	0.00	0.00	1.00
2	0.09	0.09	0.13	0.24	0.22	0.12	0.06	0.03	0.02	0.01	0.00	0.00	0.00	0.97
3	0.09	0.09	0.13	0.22	0.22	0.12	0.06	0.03	0.02	0.01	0.00	0.00	0.01	0.98
4	0.10	0.09	0.13	0.21	0.21	0.12	0.07	0.03	0.02	0.01	0.01	0.00	0.01	0.98
Non-serious casualty														
1	0.05	0.07	0.13	0.25	0.22	0.11	0.06	0.03	0.02	0.01	0.01	0.01	0.03	1.14
2	0.08	0.09	0.13	0.23	0.20	0.12	0.06	0.03	0.02	0.01	0.01	0.01	0.02	1.05
3	0.08	0.10	0.13	0.20	0.20	0.12	0.07	0.04	0.02	0.01	0.01	0.01	0.01	1.05
4	0.09	0.10	0.12	0.19	0.19	0.12	0.07	0.04	0.03	0.01	0.01	0.01	0.01	1.05
Serious casualty														
1	0.02	0.04	0.11	0.21	0.17	0.11	0.06	0.05	0.04	0.02	0.02	0.02	0.13	1.65
2	0.05	0.08	0.13	0.18	0.18	0.11	0.06	0.05	0.03	0.02	0.01	0.01	0.08	1.46
3	0.06	0.08	0.12	0.17	0.19	0.13	0.06	0.05	0.04	0.02	0.02	0.01	0.04	1.24
4	0.05	0.08	0.12	0.17	0.18	0.14	0.09	0.05	0.04	0.02	0.01	0.01	0.03	1.22
Very serious casualty														
1	0.01	0.01	0.05	0.12	0.13	0.08	0.05	0.04	0.03	0.05	0.03	0.04	0.37	2.80
2	0.03	0.06	0.07	0.12	0.16	0.14	0.10	0.07	0.02	0.03	0.03	0.02	0.14	1.81
3	0.03	0.05	0.09	0.14	0.15	0.13	0.14	0.06	0.05	0.02	0.03	0.02	0.09	1.59
4	0.03	0.04	0.08	0.11	0.15	0.16	0.12	0.09	0.05	0.04	0.02	0.02	0.08	1.54

Table B.2
Distribution of Estimated Replacement Rates, Excluding TSGLI Income, by Injury Type and Years Since Deployment: AC

Injury Type/ Years Since Deployment	Replacement Rate (percent)													Mean Rep. Rate
	0–25	25–50	50–75	75–100	100–125	125–150	150–175	175–200	200–225	225–250	250–275	275–300	300+	
Uninjured														
1	0.04	0.05	0.11	0.29	0.27	0.12	0.06	0.03	0.01	0.01	0.00	0.00	0.00	1.04
2	0.06	0.06	0.12	0.25	0.24	0.13	0.06	0.03	0.02	0.01	0.01	0.00	0.01	1.03
3	0.08	0.07	0.12	0.23	0.23	0.13	0.07	0.03	0.02	0.01	0.01	0.00	0.01	1.03
4	0.10	0.07	0.12	0.21	0.22	0.13	0.07	0.04	0.02	0.01	0.01	0.00	0.01	1.02
Self-reported														
1	0.05	0.07	0.12	0.27	0.26	0.12	0.06	0.02	0.01	0.01	0.00	0.00	0.00	1.01
2	0.08	0.08	0.12	0.23	0.23	0.12	0.06	0.03	0.02	0.01	0.01	0.00	0.01	1.00
3	0.10	0.08	0.12	0.22	0.22	0.12	0.06	0.03	0.02	0.01	0.00	0.00	0.01	0.99
4	0.11	0.09	0.12	0.20	0.21	0.12	0.07	0.03	0.02	0.01	0.01	0.00	0.01	0.99
Referred														
1	0.06	0.07	0.12	0.27	0.25	0.12	0.05	0.03	0.01	0.01	0.00	0.00	0.00	1.00
2	0.09	0.09	0.13	0.24	0.22	0.12	0.06	0.03	0.02	0.01	0.00	0.00	0.00	0.97
3	0.09	0.09	0.13	0.22	0.22	0.12	0.06	0.03	0.02	0.01	0.00	0.00	0.01	0.98
4	0.10	0.09	0.13	0.21	0.21	0.12	0.07	0.03	0.02	0.01	0.01	0.00	0.01	0.98
Non-serious casualty														
1	0.05	0.07	0.14	0.26	0.23	0.12	0.06	0.03	0.02	0.01	0.00	0.00	0.01	1.02
2	0.08	0.10	0.13	0.23	0.21	0.12	0.06	0.03	0.02	0.01	0.01	0.00	0.01	1.01
3	0.08	0.10	0.13	0.20	0.20	0.12	0.07	0.04	0.02	0.01	0.01	0.01	0.01	1.04
4	0.09	0.10	0.12	0.19	0.19	0.12	0.07	0.04	0.03	0.01	0.01	0.01	0.01	1.05
Serious casualty														
1	0.02	0.05	0.13	0.27	0.22	0.14	0.07	0.04	0.02	0.01	0.01	0.01	0.01	1.10
2	0.05	0.09	0.15	0.21	0.20	0.12	0.07	0.05	0.03	0.01	0.01	0.01	0.01	1.10
3	0.06	0.08	0.13	0.18	0.20	0.13	0.06	0.05	0.04	0.02	0.02	0.01	0.02	1.17
4	0.05	0.08	0.12	0.17	0.18	0.15	0.09	0.05	0.04	0.02	0.01	0.01	0.03	1.20
Very serious casualty														
1	0.01	0.03	0.09	0.21	0.25	0.17	0.10	0.04	0.02	0.02	0.01	0.01	0.03	1.27
2	0.03	0.06	0.09	0.15	0.20	0.16	0.11	0.07	0.03	0.02	0.02	0.01	0.05	1.35
3	0.03	0.05	0.10	0.14	0.15	0.14	0.14	0.07	0.05	0.02	0.03	0.02	0.07	1.48
4	0.03	0.04	0.08	0.11	0.15	0.17	0.12	0.09	0.05	0.04	0.02	0.02	0.07	1.51

Table B.3
Distribution of Estimated Replacement Rates, Including TSGLI Income, by Injury Type and Years Since Deployment: RC

Injury Type/ Years Since Deployment	Replacement Rate (percent)													Mean Rep. Rate
	0–25	25–50	50–75	75–100	100–125	125–150	150–175	175–200	200–225	225–250	250–275	275–300	300+	
Uninjured														
1	0.05	0.07	0.12	0.29	0.25	0.10	0.05	0.03	0.02	0.01	0.01	0.00	0.01	1.06
2	0.05	0.07	0.13	0.27	0.24	0.10	0.05	0.03	0.02	0.01	0.01	0.00	0.01	1.05
3	0.06	0.06	0.13	0.26	0.24	0.11	0.06	0.03	0.02	0.01	0.01	0.00	0.01	1.04
4	0.08	0.07	0.13	0.24	0.23	0.11	0.06	0.03	0.02	0.01	0.01	0.00	0.01	1.05
Self-reported														
1	0.06	0.07	0.12	0.28	0.24	0.10	0.05	0.03	0.02	0.01	0.01	0.01	0.02	1.01
2	0.06	0.07	0.12	0.27	0.23	0.10	0.05	0.03	0.02	0.01	0.01	0.01	0.02	0.97
3	0.07	0.07	0.13	0.24	0.22	0.11	0.06	0.03	0.02	0.01	0.01	0.01	0.01	1.07
4	0.08	0.07	0.12	0.22	0.22	0.12	0.06	0.03	0.02	0.01	0.01	0.01	0.01	1.07
Referred														
1	0.05	0.07	0.12	0.28	0.25	0.10	0.05	0.03	0.02	0.01	0.01	0.01	0.02	1.10
2	0.05	0.07	0.13	0.27	0.24	0.11	0.05	0.03	0.02	0.01	0.01	0.00	0.02	1.08
3	0.06	0.07	0.12	0.25	0.23	0.11	0.06	0.03	0.02	0.01	0.01	0.00	0.02	1.09
4	0.07	0.07	0.13	0.23	0.22	0.12	0.06	0.03	0.02	0.01	0.01	0.01	0.02	1.09
Non-serious casualty														
1	0.05	0.07	0.12	0.22	0.22	0.11	0.06	0.04	0.02	0.02	0.01	0.01	0.05	1.28
2	0.05	0.07	0.12	0.23	0.22	0.12	0.07	0.04	0.02	0.01	0.01	0.00	0.02	1.15
3	0.06	0.08	0.12	0.21	0.22	0.13	0.07	0.04	0.02	0.02	0.01	0.01	0.02	1.13
4	0.06	0.08	0.11	0.19	0.21	0.13	0.08	0.05	0.03	0.02	0.01	0.01	0.02	1.14
Serious casualty														
1	0.03	0.04	0.09	0.19	0.20	0.09	0.06	0.03	0.03	0.03	0.03	0.01	0.16	1.86
2	0.02	0.05	0.10	0.20	0.19	0.12	0.07	0.03	0.03	0.03	0.02	0.01	0.12	1.88
3	0.04	0.05	0.13	0.14	0.23	0.13	0.11	0.05	0.02	0.03	0.02	0.02	0.04	1.42
4	0.04	0.03	0.12	0.19	0.18	0.14	0.08	0.06	0.05	0.03	0.02	0.01	0.04	1.43
Very serious casualty														
1	0.02	0.02	0.05	0.09	0.11	0.05	0.04	0.07	0.04	0.04	0.04	0.01	0.45	4.42
2	0.03	0.02	0.07	0.11	0.08	0.15	0.05	0.10	0.07	0.07	0.03	0.03	0.20	2.13
3	0.02	0.05	0.04	0.15	0.15	0.11	0.15	0.09	0.03	0.05	0.01	0.02	0.12	1.82
4	0.03	0.04	0.07	0.11	0.15	0.11	0.14	0.08	0.06	0.07	0.02	0.00	0.15	1.83

Table B.4
Distribution of Estimated Replacement Rates, Excluding TSGLI Income, by Injury Type and Years Since Deployment: RC

Injury Type/ Years Since Deployment	Replacement Rate (percent)													Mean Rep. Rate
	0–25	25–50	50–75	75–100	100–125	125–150	150–175	175–200	200–225	225–250	250–275	275–300	300+	
Uninjured														
1	0.05	0.07	0.12	0.29	0.25	0.10	0.05	0.03	0.02	0.01	0.01	0.00	0.01	1.06
2	0.05	0.07	0.13	0.27	0.24	0.10	0.05	0.03	0.02	0.01	0.01	0.00	0.01	1.05
3	0.06	0.06	0.13	0.26	0.24	0.11	0.06	0.03	0.02	0.01	0.01	0.00	0.01	1.04
4	0.08	0.07	0.13	0.24	0.23	0.11	0.06	0.03	0.02	0.01	0.01	0.00	0.01	1.04
Self-reported														
1	0.06	0.07	0.12	0.28	0.24	0.10	0.05	0.03	0.02	0.01	0.01	0.01	0.02	1.11
2	0.06	0.07	0.12	0.27	0.23	0.10	0.05	0.03	0.02	0.01	0.01	0.00	0.02	1.07
3	0.07	0.07	0.13	0.24	0.22	0.11	0.06	0.03	0.02	0.01	0.01	0.01	0.01	1.06
4	0.08	0.07	0.12	0.22	0.22	0.12	0.06	0.03	0.02	0.01	0.01	0.01	0.01	1.07
Referred														
1	0.05	0.07	0.12	0.28	0.25	0.10	0.05	0.03	0.02	0.01	0.01	0.01	0.02	1.09
2	0.05	0.07	0.12	0.27	0.24	0.11	0.05	0.03	0.02	0.01	0.01	0.01	0.02	1.12
3	0.06	0.07	0.12	0.25	0.23	0.11	0.06	0.03	0.02	0.01	0.01	0.00	0.02	1.09
4	0.07	0.07	0.13	0.23	0.22	0.12	0.06	0.04	0.02	0.01	0.01	0.01	0.02	1.09
Non-serious casualty														
1	0.05	0.07	0.12	0.22	0.22	0.11	0.06	0.04	0.02	0.02	0.01	0.01	0.05	1.28
2	0.05	0.07	0.12	0.23	0.22	0.12	0.07	0.04	0.02	0.01	0.01	0.00	0.02	1.15
3	0.06	0.08	0.12	0.21	0.22	0.13	0.07	0.04	0.02	0.02	0.01	0.01	0.02	1.13
4	0.06	0.08	0.11	0.19	0.21	0.13	0.08	0.05	0.03	0.02	0.01	0.01	0.02	1.14
Serious casualty														
1	0.03	0.05	0.11	0.22	0.22	0.12	0.08	0.05	0.02	0.02	0.03	0.00	0.06	0.34
2	0.03	0.05	0.10	0.21	0.23	0.15	0.08	0.04	0.03	0.01	0.02	0.01	0.04	1.40
3	0.04	0.05	0.13	0.14	0.23	0.13	0.11	0.05	0.01	0.03	0.02	0.01	0.04	1.39
4	0.04	0.03	0.13	0.19	0.19	0.15	0.08	0.06	0.04	0.03	0.02	0.01	0.04	1.39
Very serious casualty														
1	0.02	0.02	0.07	0.13	0.19	0.09	0.06	0.09	0.05	0.08	0.04	0.04	0.13	1.87
2	0.02	0.02	0.09	0.14	0.10	0.16	0.08	0.13	0.05	0.06	0.01	0.03	0.10	1.71
3	0.02	0.05	0.05	0.15	0.15	0.11	0.15	0.08	0.03	0.06	0.01	0.02	0.11	1.68
4	0.03	0.04	0.08	0.13	0.15	0.10	0.12	0.08	0.07	0.07	0.02	0.00	0.13	1.72

**Figure B.1
Histogram of Estimated Replacement Rates Including TSGLI Income for AC Members, by
Injury Type**

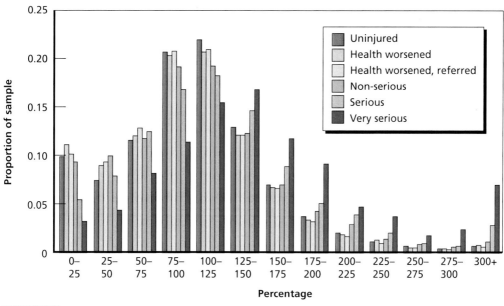

RAND *MG1166-B.1*

**Figure B.2
Histogram of Estimated Replacement Rates Including TSGLI Income for RC Members, by
Injury Type**

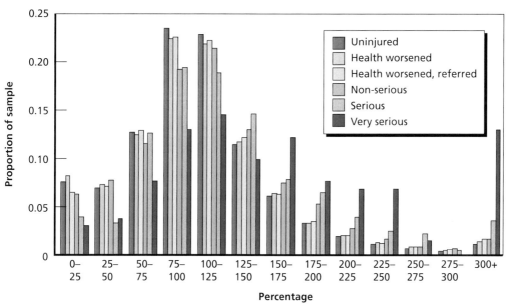

RAND *MG1166-B.2*

References

Angrist, Joshua D., "Lifetime Earnings and the Vietnam Era Draft Lottery: Evidence from Social Security Administrative Records," *The American Economic Review*, Vol. 80, No. 1, 1990, pp. 313–335.

———, "Estimating the Labor Market Impact of Voluntary Military Service Using Social Security Data on Military Applicants," *Econometrica,* Vol. 66, No. 2, 1998, pp. 249–288.

Angrist, Joshua D., and John H. Johnson, "Effects of Work-Related Absences on Families: Evidence from the Gulf War," *Industrial and Labor Relations Review*, Vol. 54, No. 1, 2000, pp. 41–58.

Bound, John, "Self-Reported Versus Objective Measures of Health in Retirement Models," *Journal of Human Resources*, Vol. 26, 1991, pp. 107–137.

Bound, John, and Richard Burkhauser, "Economic Analysis of Transfer Programs Targeted on People with Disabilities," in Orley Ashenfelter and David Card (eds.), *Handbook of Labor Economics,* Volume 3, Elsevier, 1999, pp. 3417–3528.

Buddin, Richard, and Bing Han, *Is Military Disability Compensation Adequate to Offset Civilian Earnings Loss from Service-Connected Disabilities?* Santa Monica, Calif.: RAND Corporation, unpublished working paper, 2011.

Buddin, Richard, and Kanika Kapur, *An Analysis of Military Disability Compensation*, Santa Monica, Calif.: RAND Corporation, MG-369-OSD, 2005. As of September 19, 2011:
http://www.rand.org/pubs/monographs/MG369.html

Chandra, Anita, Sandraluz Lara-Cinisomo, Lisa H. Jaycox, Terri Tanielian, Rachel M. Burns, Teague Ruder, and Bing Han, "Children on the Homefront: The Experience of Children from Military Families," *Pediatrics*, Vol. 125, No. 1, 2010, pp. 16–25.

Christensen, Eric, Candace Hill, Pat Netzer, DeAnn Farr, Elizabeth Schaefer, and Joyce McMahon, *Economic Impact on Caregivers of the Seriously Wounded, Ill, and Injured*, Alexandria, Va.: Center for Naval Analyses, 2009.

Christensen, Eric, Joyce McMahon, Elizabeth Schaefer, Ted Jaditz, and Dan Harris, *Final Report for the Veterans' Disability Benefits Commission: Compensation, Survey Results, and Selected Topics*, Alexandria, Va.: Center for Naval Analyses, 2007.

Defense Manpower Data Center, "Military Casualty Information," web page, undated. As of May 20, 2011:
http://siadapp.dmdc.osd.mil/personnel/CASUALTY/castop.htm

EconSys, *A Study of Compensation Payments for Service-Connected Disabilities*, Falls Church, Va., 2008.

GAO—*See* U.S. Government Accountability Office.

Greenberg, Greg, and Robert Rosenheck, "Compensation of Veterans with Psychiatric or Substance Abuse Disorders and Employment and Earnings," *Military Medicine*, Vol. 172, No. 2, 2007, pp. 162–168.

Gronau, Reuben, "Leisure, Home Production, and Work—The Theory of the Allocation of Time Revisited," *Journal of Political Economy*, Vol. 85, No. 6, 1977, pp. 1099–1123.

Heaton, Paul, and David S. Loughran, "Post-Traumatic Stress Disorder and the Earnings of Military Reservists," Santa Monica, Calif.: RAND Corporation, unpublished working paper, 2011.

Hoge, C. W., C. A. Castro, S. C. Messer, D. McGurk, D., et al., "Combat Duty in Iraq and Afghanistan, Mental Health Problems, and Barriers to Care," *New England Journal of Medicine*, Vol. 351, No. 1, 2004, pp. 13–22.

Hosek, James R., *How Is Deployment to Iraq and Afghanistan Affecting U.S. Service Members and Their Families? An Overview of Early RAND Research on the Topic*, Santa Monica, Calif.: RAND Corporation, OP-316-OSD, 2011. As of September 19, 2011: http://www.rand.org/pubs/occasional_papers/OP316.html

Hosek, James R., and Paco Martorell, *How Have Deployments During the War on Terrorism Affected Reenlistment?* Santa Monica, Calif.: RAND Corporation, MG-873-OSD, 2009. As of September 19, 2011: http://www.rand.org/pubs/monographs/MG873.html

Hosek, James, Jennifer Erin Kavanagh, and Laura L. Miller, *How Deployments Affect Service Members*, Santa Monica, Calif.: RAND Corporation, MG-432-RC, 2006. As of September 19, 2011; http://www.rand.org/pubs/monographs/MG432.html

Joint Chiefs of Staff, Office of the Chairman, "Updated Procedures for Deployment Health Surveillance and Readiness," Memorandum MCM-0006-02, February 1, 2002.

Karney, Benjamin R., and John S. Crown, *Families Under Stress: An Assessment of Data, Theory, and Research on Marriage and Divorce in the Military*, Santa Monica, Calif.: RAND Corporation, MG-599-OSD, 2007. As of September 19, 2011: http://www.rand.org/pubs/monographs/MG599.html

Loughran, David S., and Jacob Alex Klerman. "The Effect of Activation on the Post-Activation Civilian Earnings of Reservists," *Labour Economics*, 2011. As of June 25, 2011: http://www.sciencedirect.com/science/article/pii/S0927537111000686

Loughran, David S., Jacob Alex Klerman, and Craig Martin, *Activation and the Earnings of Reservists*, Santa Monica, Calif.: RAND Corporation, MG-474-OSD, 2006. As of September 19, 2011: http://www.rand.org/pubs/monographs/MG474.html

Loughran, David S., Francisco Martorell, Trey Miller, and Jacob Alex Klerman, *The Effect of the Military Enlistment on Earnings and Education*, Santa Monica, Calif.: RAND Corporation, TR-995-A, 2011. As of September 26, 2011: http://www.rand.org/pubs/technical_reports/TR995.html

Lyle, David S., "Using Military Deployments and Job Assignments to Estimate the Effect of Parental Absences and Household Relocations on Children's Academic Achievement," *Journal of Labor Economics*, Vol. 24, No. 2, 2006, pp. 319–350.

Maestas, Nicole, Kathleen J. Mullen, and Alexander Strand, *Does Disability Insurance Receipt Discourage Work? Using Examiner Assignment to Estimate Causal Effects of SSDI Receipt*, Santa Monica, CA: RAND Corporation, WR-853-2, 2011. As of September 19, 2011: http://www.rand.org/pubs/working_papers/WR853-2.html

McFarlane, A. C., "Posttraumatic Stress Disorder: A Model of the Longitudinal Course and the Role of Risk Factors," *Journal of Clinical Psychiatry*, Vol. 61 (suppl. 5), 2000, pp. 15–20.

Military.com, "Special Monthly Compensation (SMC) Tables," web page, undated. As of September 15, 2011;
http://www.military.com/benefits/content/veteran-benefits/special-monthly-compensation-smc-tables.html

Mincer, Jacob, *Schooling, Experience, and Earnings*, New York: Columbia University Press, 1974.

Milliken, C. S., J. L. Auchterlonie, and C. W. Hoge, "Longitudinal Assessment of Mental Health Problems Among Active and Reserve Component Soldiers Returning From the Iraq War," *Journal of the American Medical Association*, Vol. 298, No. 18, 2007, pp. 2141–2148.

NASI—*See* National Academy of Social Insurance.

National Academy of Social Insurance, *Adequacy of Earnings Replacement in Workers' Compensation Programs*, Kalamazoo, Mich.: W. E. Upjohn Institute for Employment Research, 2004.

Negrusa, Sebastian, Brighita Negrusa, and James R. Hosek, "Effect of Work-Related Absences on Marital Stability: The Case of Recent U.S. Deployments," Santa Monica, Calif.: RAND Corporation, unpublished working paper, undated.

Office of Inspector General, *Disability Claims Overall Processing Times*, Washington, D.C.: Social Security Administration, Audit Report A-01-08-18011, 2008.

Reville, Robert T., Leslie I. Boden, Jeffrey E. Biddle, and Christopher Mardesich, *An Evaluation of New Mexico Workers' Compensation Permanent Partial Disability and Return to Work*, Santa Monica, Calif.: RAND Corporation, MR-1414-ICJ, 2001. As of September 19, 2011:
http://www.rand.org/pubs/monograph_reports/MR1414.html

Savych, Bogdan, *Effects of Deployments on Spouses of Military Personnel*, Santa Monica, Calif.: RAND Corporation, RGSD-233, 2008. As of September 19, 2011:
http://www.rand.org/pubs/rgs_dissertations/RGSD233.html

Seabury, Seth A., *Public Safety v. Private Risk: Optimal Injury Compensation for Law Enforcement Officers*, New York: Columbia University, Department of Economics, Ph.D. Dissertation, 2002.

Seabury, Seth, Robert Reville, Stephanie Williamson, Christopher F. Mclaren, Adam Gailey, Elizabeth Wilke, and Frank Neuhauser, *Workers' Compensation Reform and Return to Work: The California Experience*, Santa Monica, Calif.: RAND Corporation, MG-1035-CHSWC, 2011. As of September 19, 2011:
http://www.rand.org/pubs/monographs/MG1035.html

Social Security Online, "Code of Federal Regulations, Part 404—Federal Old-Age, Survivors and Disability Insurance (1950–)," web page, undated. As of September 15, 2011:
http://www.ssa.gov/OP_Home/cfr20/404/404-0000.htm

Tanielian, Terri, and Lisa H. Jaycox (eds.), *Invisible Wounds of War: Psychological and Cognitive Injuries, Their Consequences, and Services to Assist Recovery*, Santa Monica, Calif.: RAND Corporation, MG-720-CCF, 2008. As of September 19, 2011:
http://www.rand.org/pubs/monographs/MG720.html

"TSGLI Schedule of Losses," web page, undated. As of September 15, 2011:
http://www.insurance.va.gov/sglisite/tsgli/Schedule/Schedule.htm

U.S. Government Accountability Office, "Social Security Disability: Additional Outreach and Collaboration on Sharing Medical Records Would Improve Wounded Warrior's Access to Benefits," Report to the Subcommittee on Social Security, Committee on Ways and Means, House of Representatives, September 2009.

Werber, Laura, Margaret C. Harrell, Danielle M. Varda, Kimberly Curry Hall, Megan K. Becket, and Stefanie Stern, *Deployment Experiences of Guard and Reserve Families: Implications for Support and Retention*, Santa Monica, Calif.: RAND Corporation, MG-645-OSD, 2008. As of September 19, 2011:
http://www.rand.org/pubs/monographs/MG645.html